Against the Odds

Dedicated to the memory of my mother, Mairead.

BRIAN CROWLEY

AGAINST THE ODDS

A BIOGRAPHY BY BREDA JOY

First published in 1996 by
Brandon Book Publishers Ltd
Dingle, Co. Kerry, Ireland.

British Library Cataloguing in Publication Data is available
for this book.

ISBN 0 86322 223 4

The publishers are grateful to Bardis Music Co. for permission to
reproduce 'Summer in Dublin' by Liam O'Reilly
Cover photography by Barry Murphy, Foto Works, Tralee;
author photograph by Valerie O'Sullivan
Cover designed by Peter Staunton, Design Gang, Tralee
Typeset by Elaine Garvey, Dingle
Printed by Colour Books Ltd, Dublin

Acknowledgements

Many people helped to fill out the picture of Brian Crowley presented here, and I thank them for their time and encouragement, especially John Cushnahan MEP who responded so promptly to a request for an interview, and not least Brian Crowley himself, who submitted to my questioning for many months. A number of people helped to make this book possible by providing me with back-up and support. They include Peter Malone and Manus O'Callaghan, who chased up so many of the interviewees, and Bríd Leahy and Anne Pullen who typed many pages of interview transcripts. Finally, special thanks is due to my friends and family, to the Herlihy family, and to my son, Brendan, for being so patient.

Prologue

A S THE BIG Opel Rekord moved through the night towards Clonakilty, its headlights searching the bends of the West Cork roads and the wipers swishing a comforting rhythm on the windscreen, eight-year-old Brian snuggled into the passenger seat. It was Friday night. Next week would bring school and homework and the train that took his daddy away to Dublin, but now there were just the two of them and the excitement of the world of big people ahead.

Flor Crowley nudged the small form sitting beside him. 'You're some bloody man, Brian boy!' Brian grinned back at him in the darkness.

A big-framed, heavy man with eyes that creased when he smiled, Brian's father looked larger than ever under the low ceiling of Shanley's as he lit his trademark cigar and greeted the men in the bar. The legs of the wooden stool creaked on the concrete floor as he pulled it up to the counter. 'What's the news in Clonakilty this week, Delia?' he enquired of the woman behind the counter.

Flor Crowley was a public man, a Fianna Fáil politician representing the constituency of Mid-Cork in the Dáil. When the week's parliamentary business was done, he left the city and headed home, to spend the next three days and nights meeting his constituents at clinics held in the back rooms of pubs and small hotels throughout West Cork. Clonakilty, Skibbereen and

Dunmanway were the venues for weekly clinics, and he visited Castletownbere in the farthest corner of the straggling constituency on alternate Fridays, taking in clinics in Glengariff and Bantry on the same day. Saturdays were spent in his constituency office in Bandon. Then there were constituency meetings and socials to attend.

Flor loved to bring his son with him as he toured the small towns of West Cork. He would have brought all six of his children if he could, but Brian was the only one who was eager to go. In the dimly lit pub in Clonakilty, Delia Shanley took Brian under her wing. She was fond of Flor Crowley and all his family, especially young Brian. He had a golden head of curls and a lovely quick smile, and he had a pair of eyes which never missed a thing; she noticed that particularly.

Delia reserved her best room for special occasions – for Christmas and the Stations, and for Flor Crowley's clinic. She was a diehard Fianna Fáil supporter. Her husband voted Fine Gael though, and while he observed the ritual of polling day by dressing in his best suit and going faithfully to cast his vote, Patrick Shanley would often remark wryly that there was little point in the exercise as he and his wife just cancelled each other out.

They ran the pub together and it also spoke of the political idiosyncrasies of the Cork countryside. It dated from 1903, when Patrick Shanley's father sniffed trouble on the wind and applied for an early discharge from the Royal Irish Constabulary. He travelled to London to have his application heard and received a royal gratuity with his discharge papers. The queen's gold helped pay for the pub, but through the troubled years of the War of Independence the Shanley sympathies were firmly republican, and members of Tom Barry's flying column were often sheltered in a false room concealed in the attic. One of Barry's Volunteers was Flor Crowley's uncle, shot and killed in December 1921.

Flor sat behind the table in Delia Shanley's best room as his constituents came in to ask his help and advice: an unemployed man who had been refused social welfare; a couple with five children whose application for a council house had been delayed once again; a farmer who had failed to get a grant for new machinery; a father wondering if the TD could put in a word for his son who was looking for a job in the county council. Flor made notes of their circumstances and promised to intervene on their behalf. Solving these bread and butter problems was the stuff of a political career, but the TD also heard of more personal concerns, about family conflicts, arguments over land, individual worries about the future. 'Confessions' his family called them, and that, Flor reflected, was what his clinics often resembled.

Brian sat outside in the pub where the talk was of cattle and crops, the fortunes of Cork hurling and the fist Jack Lynch was making of the country. As the night wore on, fields were ploughed and crops sown on the counter of the bar. A haze of Sweet Afton and Woodbine cigarette smoke hung heavily in the air. Delia came out from behind the counter to check on her young charge. His eyes were dimmed with tiredness, but he was not the least daunted by the crowd and sat there sipping orange, absorbing the scene around him. 'Your father won't be long more,' Delia assured the boy as she gathered some glasses off the table. 'Would you like to go for election some day, like your daddy?' she asked him jokingly.

Brian thought about this for a moment. 'No, I wouldn't,' he said eventually, 'because you have to ask too many people to vote for you.'

Chapter One

AS THE CROWLEYS sorted out their belongings in Craigie, their new home, Brian, just over a year old, studied the disarray from his perch on a high chair in the kitchen. It was the end of April 1965, and Flor Crowley had brought his wife and family home from Dublin to their West Cork roots.

The fine spacious old house, standing high over a sloping garden on the Dunmanway Road, represented the rising fortunes of the widow's son, who had grown up in a gatekeeper's lodge on the outskirts of Cork. His father, Jerome, a gatekeeper at the Cork Asylum, had died when Flor was eight years old, leaving his wife, Mary, with three children to raise. Mary was a nurse from Macroom, a religious woman with tremendous devotion to Our Lady, and a strong republican. She was more republican even than her husband, though his brothers had all been in the IRA during the War of Independence. When Flor went on holidays to his father's old home in Dunmanway every year, he absorbed an equal measure of religion and rebellion from his uncles. As they milked the cows in the evening, the two older men would recite the rosary between them, and later they would swop tales of Kilmichael, Upton, Crossbarry and the other ambushes that took place in West Cork during the 'Troubles'.

When friends of Flor's took over Bandon Mills, he was invited to return to Cork to join the company as manager. Bandon was a plantation town in the heartland of a rich, agricultural plain.

The presence of three banks – the Munster and Leinster, the Bank of Ireland and the Provincial – was testimony to its solid standing. The town had been developed in the early 1600s by the first Earl of Cork, Richard Boyle, who had induced hundreds of families to come over from England to take holdings there. The settlers were mostly Puritans, and as a result of their industry the town had prospered, becoming the only walled town in West Cork. Indeed, the Earl boasted that the walls of the town were superior to those of Derry, and they functioned in much the same way: for 200 years after Bandon's foundation, no Catholic had been allowed to live there.

Times had changed, of course. Flor Crowley had spent seven years working with an American company in Dublin, selling accounting machines and advising businesses on new equipment, and the rising tide which Taoiseach Sean Lemass said would lift all boats had carried his hopes high on its swell. 'I made a lot of money in those days,' Flor acknowledges freely, 'because what we had to sell was unique. It was the beginning of the computer age. It was a fledgling industry and we were in at the start of it.'

He and his wife had enjoyed the city. Flor had been 24 and Sally a year younger when they set up home in Rathfarnham, and they had three children during their time there. Niall was born in 1960, Maeve two years later, and on 4 March 1964 Daniel Brian Crowley entered the world. The latest addition to the Crowley family was called after his maternal grandfather, Dan Collins. A big ginger-haired fellow, Dan was a popular personality, fondly remembered as 'a great man to stand to a child'. 'There's an awful lot of my father in Brian,' Sally observes. 'He was gregarious and happy and outgoing. There's a photo of my father laughing, and I can see Brian in it.'

The family moved back to Cork when Brian was six months old, staying in a house belonging to one of Sally's aunts while Flor took up his job at the mill. A few months later they bought

Craigie for £3,000. Flor jokes that he came into a political household; the previous owner had been District Justice James F. Crotty whose brother and subsequently his nephew were Fine Gael deputies for Kilkenny.

At this time, Flor and Sally had three children under the age of four, and Sally was pregnant with their fourth child. Flor had a new job and they had moved to a new home, but there were even further changes on the way. Flor decided to run in a by-election in the Mid-Cork constituency, later to become Cork South-West. Over lunchtime debates in the Munster Arms Hotel, two friends of his, Fianna Fáil supporters Dan Joe O'Mahony and Derry O'Connell, had encouraged him to go forward. Flor had a great admiration for Sean Lemass and was fired by the mood of optimism the Fianna Fáil leader was inspiring in the country. Lemass had been in the GPO during the Easter Rising, but he was breaking new ground on north-south relations in his meetings with the Prime Minister of Northern Ireland, Terence O'Neill, and promoting new economic policies aimed at modernising the Irish economy. Politics was in the Crowley family, in any case; besides his father's generation's being heavily involved in the War of Independence, his grandfather had been a member of Cork County Council.

Flor ran against Eileen Desmond of the Labour party in a by-election in March and was beaten on the third count, but the following month Sean Lemass called a general election and this time he contested the seat successfully. It was a victory tinged with sadness, however. On the night that Flor was declared a TD, Sally was in the Bon Secours Hospital in Cork where she lost the baby she had been carrying since they left Dublin.

Flor was thirty years old when he took his seat in the Dáil, in what was to be Sean Lemass's last government. In 1966 Lemass handed the leadership of Fianna Fáil to Jack Lynch, a Corkman with perhaps less ambition than the young Turks of the party whose names would become part of the lexicon of Irish politics in the years to come. Flor Crowley was a modest man, too, but he would nonetheless be caught up in the changes confronting Irish political life in the 1960s. In the meantime, shortly after he was elected Flor started an auctioneering business to supplement his Dáil salary and to provide a financial safety net for the family if things should go wrong politically.

The die was now cast for the type of family life the Crowleys would experience, a frenetic life spent always in the glare of politics. Their new home in Bandon became an open house; because so many people were always calling to see Flor, they simply left the back door open so that they could walk in. There were always aunts, uncles and cousins around. Sally's brother's family came on holiday from England, and after her brother's wife died of multiple sclerosis, they spent even more time in Craigie. And when the young Crowleys started school in Bandon and began to make friends, they were encouraged to bring home their schoolmates, who would often stay for dinner or tea.

'I always had a home where they could bring in whoever they wanted to, whenever they wanted to. Friends are really extended family: I feel very strongly about that,' Sally Crowley says. She got great joy out of being with her children and wanted to recreate some of the atmosphere of her own childhood home for them. She had been brought up on Wilton Road, a neat row of houses on the outskirts of Cork where the city yielded to green fields and country lanes. Her father was a successful, self-made man, who ran a business selling farm produce in the city and was well-known throughout West Cork from travelling the country buying poultry and eggs for export to Britain, and fish for export to Britain and the continent. 'The Collins were a very close-knit family and still are; equally so the Crowleys,' Sally remarks.

After the birth of her children Sally had become a full-time mother, and now, like all political wives, she had the responsibility of running the household on her own while her husband attended the Dáil. She ran his office from the house, taking phone calls and arranging appointments, and at weekends she regularly accompanied him to political functions. At home she extended hospitality to the diverse range of people who arrived at her door, whether West Cork farmers or political figures of the day, and when elections came round she went out into the constituency and canvassed for her husband.

With three, and then six children to deal with – Deirdre, Flor Junior and Fiona were added to the fold in the first few years in Bandon – Sally Crowley ran a tight ship. If the children stepped out of line boldly, they were sent to their rooms. The wooden spoon was taken out when it was needed. On one occasion the spoon broke when Brian was getting a slap, and he kept the pieces to show to visitors saying, 'Look what they do to me!' He was mischievous and had quite a fiery temper, and felt indignant when he was punished. However, his hurt was rarely so great that it would not quickly be forgotten. It was never punitive in the family. 'If you were told not to do something and you did do it,' Brian says, 'you were not going to be kicked out.'

Because Flor and Sally were often out at functions and political meetings, the young Crowleys were regularly minded by babysitters. Brian shared a bedroom with his young brother Flor and relations between them were for the most part fairly mixed: they spent their time skirmishing, breaking off only to rush across the landing and raid Niall's room. When Brian got angry, he'd get stuck into his older brother, even though he could never win. He gave the babysitters a hard time, too. He would insist on staying up until his parents came back, and if he was cajoled or coerced into going to bed, he would lie there forcing himself to stay awake. Once, in a fit of temper, he threatened to jump out of the upstairs window if he was sent to bed early.

As babysitters wilted before the Crowley boys' onslaught and the pressures of running a home and being a political spouse at the same time increased, Sally decided it was time to call in reinforcements on the domestic front. The family took on a housekeeper, Frances O'Callaghan, who began work when Brian was six and his baby sister Fiona was just six months. She became 'Mrs O'Callaghan' to the family, or Mocko for short. Her own four children were one age to the Crowleys, so the Crowley kids made room for them at lunch and after school. At mealtimes there were often ten children in the kitchen. 'You'd feed half of them and the other half would say, "Are we getting anything to eat?" If you had something light in the middle of the day and a dinner in the evening, we'd give them what you'd call "a walk around the table".'

Brian was the same age as Mrs O'Callaghan's Nelius, and the two boys were constantly at war, until they discovered that they had another factor to contend with. 'That is when the wooden spoon would be going to work,' Mrs O'Callaghan remembers. A forthright, plain speaking woman, she stood for no nonsense.

The Crowley household may have been strict, as was the convention of the time, but it was also a place of great fun where affection was warm and open. The children were encouraged to say their morning and night prayers, and every evening the family knelt in the kitchen to say the rosary, though sometimes an outbreak of helpless giggling from the younger ones might cause the prayers to be abandoned. The press of people who crowded the house made for a friendly, welcoming atmosphere. Slagging or baiting was practised to a fine art, and one of the liveliest artists was Mrs O'Callaghan, who especially enjoyed crossing swords with Flor Senior. Sally enjoyed singing and drama, and in the evening she would teach the children to sing or to play the piano. They would gather together for a sing-song, and Brian was soon picking up a repertoire of West Cork rebel favourites like 'The Lonely Woods of Upton'. Tall for his age and pudgy, young Brian had inherited his father's lightheartedness. A natural mimic, he would take off TV advertisements as his party piece, and when Flor's brother, Fr Pat, came to visit from England, Brian would set off after him, following solemnly in his footsteps as he made rounds of the garden reading his breviary.

Because their father was away a lot, time was precious when he was at home. On Thursday evenings the family would pile into the car and head to Cork to meet him off the train from Dublin. It was one of the highlights of the week for the children. Sally would stand on the railway platform, her baby girl in her arms, while her children fidgeted beside her, three boys and two girls holding hands and hopping from one foot to the other. Once the whistle of the approaching train was heard and its lamp shone through the tunnel, the children became more excited despite their mother's attempts to calm them. As the lighted carriages passed by like a series of film frames, they would search the windows, and then their father was on the platform, bending down to embrace the tide of children, Niall, Maeve, Deirdre, Brian and Flor Junior swinging from his coat and competing for hugs. Dropping his bags on the ground, he scooped the children up in his arms, and they squealed with delight as he swung them round.

Flor Crowley put his family first, and took every opportunity to be at home. He didn't go to Dublin a day earlier than he had to. 'In politics, you could be out every hour of the day and night. I always had an inner belief that no matter how successful you are in politics, your family is more important. In the end it's more important to be successful with them.'

In his new role as a rural TD, he threw himself into the round of public meetings and clinics with enthusiasm, but he wasn't without his critics. There were murmurings of discontent among some who felt he could be doing more for the constituency. The force of his personality, which won him the support of the West Cork voters, brought him into conflict with party activists on occasion, but in those heady early years, tensions within the organisation locally were insignificant. Travelling to meetings all along the Cork South-West constituency, stretching along the coast from Kinsale right down to Castletownbere, Flor snatched time with Sally and the children whenever he could. Even Sunday wasn't entirely a sacred day as constituents could be sure of buttonholing their TD at home after mass.

The last of the Sunday roast carved and dished out, Sally Crowley takes her own plate at the big kitchen table. The sound of cutlery clattering on dishes rises above the din of voices competing to be heard. Flor begins to quote some salacious details from an article in one of the Sunday papers but Sally cuts him short. Flor turns to the sports pages. He loves horses and promises to bring Brian to watch the horses in training at Macroom if he finishes everything on his plate. Flor has boundless enthusiasm for all sports. A photo on the kitchen wall shows him nudging in beside Lester Piggott at a race meeting in Tralee. He is addicted to crosswords. The bookcase in the front room is filled with poetry books; these belong to Sally. She likes poetry and theatre and the arts in general.

The dinner table is an open forum where everything is discussed. Every member of the family is encouraged to join in, though if anyone makes a stupid statement they are ribbed, so they learn early on to have some sense of what they are talking about. Because they are sitting around together and things get discussed a lot, the children become aware that people talk about their father because he is in public life. He was even rumoured to have died once, and the family received phone calls of sympathy. The Sunday sessions are a great forum for debate and for slagging, but also a forum where the children pick up on currents from the world outside.

Today's noisy clamour is interrupted by a knock at the back door. Fiona answers it and skips back into the room, saying there's a man looking for Daddy. Flor rolls his eyes to heaven and mutters a profanity. Sally throws him a stern look and goes to the door. No, he isn't intruding at all, she assures the caller.

They were just finishing. Flor would be with him in a minute.

The procession of people arriving at Craigie was part and parcel of growing up for the Crowley children. Today, it could be a Council tenant in arrears with rent. Tomorrow, it could be a political figure. And when 'important people' called, Brian and his brothers and sisters were in the midst of them. 'It wasn't as if we were all just stood in line at the door and introduced to them. If they were coming for dinner, we'd all be sitting around the same table.' Yet there was a sense that these were important people, 'not so much because they were friends of my father's or that they were politicians, but that they were people with responsibility'.

Brian and his brothers and sisters met many figures from the political arena in the house on the Dunmanway Road. Ray McSharry was a regular visitor. Like Flor, he was a non-drinker and was rearing a family of six, and the two men often fell into each other's company in Dublin, preferring to go to a match or to the cinema rather than to the pub. McSharry sat in occasionally on the card sessions which Brian's grandmother, Mary Crowley, started when she came to live in Bandon in her final years. She taught her grandchildren the intricacies of thirty-five and Don, a game peculiar to Cork. Brian Lenihan and Albert Reynold were other visitors to the house. Charlie Haughey gave Brian his first decimal coin, a fifty pence piece, when the 'new money' was introduced in 1971.

Every summer the Collins' old holiday home in Youghal became a rallying point for the Crowley and Collins clans. Dan Collins would take the whole gang of children on drives through the countryside in his black Ford V8. On Sunday mornings he treated them to orange and crisps while he had a pint in Moby Dick's, the pub named after the whale when scenes from *Moby Dick* had been filmed in the town. There was swimming, picnics, football on the beach, and in the evening the 'hurdy-gurdies' at Perks' Funfair. Later memories of Youghal took on an aura of sadness when Dan Collins became ill. The strength slowly ebbed away from the big, genial man, for so long the heart and soul of their holidays. He died on 6 August 1972, when Brian was eight years old.

Other family holidays were spent in Donegal. In the evening, when they gathered in the lounge with other holidaymakers, Brian was always the first one up to sing, and would launch into his favourite, Cliff Richard's Eurovision hit, 'Power to All Our Friends'. Even on holiday the family lived in a political milieu, staying at Senator Paddy McGowan's hotel in Dungloe. The company would include the McSharrys, Noel Lemass, the son of Sean Lemass, SDLP MPs John Hume, Paddy Devlin, Ivan Cooper and Seamus Mallon, and Fr Denis Faul. Just a few miles away was the north, six counties in a state of insurrection. As the kids played on the beach and chased one another into the water, they would hear snatches from the grown-ups' talk about what was happening 'across the way'. The adult conversation didn't mean much to the youngsters, but events on the other side of the border were soon to impinge on their lives in a very real and immediate manner.

YOUTHS hurling missiles, soldiers charging with batons and shields: the flickering images of rioting on the streets of Belfast and Derry flooded the safe, warm world of the Crowleys' sitting-room. The high jinks and playing stopped as the family turned shocked, solemn eyes to the television. The air of threat and menace was so strong it made a deep impression even on the young children.

On 30 January 1972, blood stained the streets of Derry, settling like shadows around the bodies of the men shot by British paratroopers, who had opened fire on a civil rights march. Those television images of bodies lying on the streets and a priest, later to become Bishop Edward Daly, holding up a white handkerchief as the wounded were carried to safety, entered homes all round the world. As distant as the street carnage seemed in one sense, Bloody Sunday was to become a catalyst which changed the course of Flor Crowley's political career and had lasting repercussions on the safe, protected home life at Craigie.

Flor Crowley travelled north with his colleague David Andrews TD for the funerals of those killed by the Paras. The day in Derry was an experience he would never forget. The IRA policed the Bogside, acting as stewards of the huge crowd which thronged the church and the route to the graveyard. They helped the southern TDs to find a parking space.

Like many people in the south, Flor Crowley was deeply troubled by events in the Six Counties. He saw the nationalists as an undefended people, without arms, facing the RUC, the British army and the infamous B Specials, a heavily armed and sectarian security militia. After Bloody Sunday he took a political decision. Angry at the way the British were behaving in the north and unhappy with Jack Lynch's handling of the situation, Crowley moved to the 'green' wing of Fianna Fáil, represented by Charles Haughey, Harry Boland and Neil Blaney, men who seemed willing to pursue the party's republican principles with more conviction. But the republican *putsch*, such as it was, ended infamously when in May 1972 Charles Haughey and Neil Blaney were charged with conspiracy to import arms illegally into the state. The charges against Blaney were soon dropped and Haughey was later acquitted, but these dramatic events sparked off bitter strife within Fianna Fáil. Boland accused Taoiseach Jack Lynch of 'felon-setting' and sought a special conference of the Fianna Fáil party to oust him. In Leinster House, Flor Crowley sided with Haughey, Blaney and Boland. He felt that northern Catholics *should* have been given arms to defend themselves. He would have favoured a peaceful solution to the northern crisis if one could have been found, but he saw no such option available just then.

When the attempt to remove Jack Lynch failed, the Cork TD's stand against Lynch, for whom he had previously voted as party leader, became an act of political suicide. Haughey was banished to the back-benches and Blaney left the party; Flor Crowley could not expect to have his way paved in the future.

In West Cork, many Fianna Fáil constituency workers and *cumainn* thought their TD's decision not to support Lynch was divisive. It was expected of people in the parliamentary party that they would give their full support to the leadership, particularly at such a critical time for the country – and a majority of people felt that the country was lucky to have had Jack Lynch in charge just then.

The strain between the republican and the moderate elements within Fianna Fáil was evident in the national context also. In the north there was a revived, armed republican force intent on bringing down the northern state; many felt that the southern state was also threatened, or that the violence up north would disrupt the social and economic development taking place in the south. Stiff measures were introduced to combat the threat to the state's security. Censorship was introduced, banning republican spokesmen from the national airwaves. The police were given special powers of arrest and detention. Phones were tapped. Flor Crowley had no doubts that his phone was tapped. 'When I realised that it was being tapped, I fed them plenty of business which wouldn't make their listening too dull.'

But in areas like West Cork, republicanism was part of the fabric of life, and echoes of 1921 and 1922, though muted, still hung in the air. Brian sensed the republican timbre. He learned the folklore of republicanism in his family's kitchen and from neighbours. Only a generation back, his uncle, Tadhg Crowley, had died alongside the parish priest of Dunmanway in a hail of Black and Tan bullets on 'a day of sunshine and hard frost'. The landmarks of republicanism lay all around them. Brian went with his father and Dan Joe O'Mahony to commemoration ceremonies at Kilmichael, Upton and Crossbarry, the scenes of fighting in the 1920s, historic place names on the map of West Cork. Dan Joe O'Mahony's family home at Belrose in Upton, a big old Georgian house, had been the headquarters of the Third West Cork Brigade during the War of Independence, and was burned down by the Black and Tans in 1921.

As a pipe band led the march down to the grey, stone monument at edge of the crossroads village of Crossbarry, Brian watched his father climb up on the lorry with Labhrás Ó Murchú of Conradh na Gaeilge and the broadcaster Prionsias Mac Aonghusa. The narrow road was crammed with people. Crossbarry had been one of the IRA's most successful ambushes during the War of Independence, but, fifty years on, the Provisional IRA was a subversive organisation. The young boy saw plainclothes Special Branch officers photographing people who had gathered at the site. He noticed that they were taking names. There was a sense of subversion just in being there, in making a statement about what you believed. The mood at ceremonies commemorating those older times was unchanged – the British had to go – but the issues were clouded by confusing messages. Republicanism was venerated by some, while others spoke of it as if it were a dirty word.

The real drift of support from Flor Crowley became apparent in the local elections of 1974, when Joe Walsh, his director of elections, left the Crowley camp, taking key people with him. Walsh was elected to Cork County Council, and now sought the Fianna Fáil nomination for the general election. There was a second name on the ballot sheet, and Walsh began to gather support at grassroots as well as organisational level, cutting into the Crowley vote. After the party lost the 1974 general election, divisions within the party locally grew acute. Dan Joe O'Mahony, one of those who first approached Flor Crowley in the Munster Arms Hotel to run as TD, was to canvass eventually for Joe Walsh. 'Let's put it this way,' he recalls. 'Joe Walsh saw what was happening quicker than anybody. He could see Flor slipping. And I don't think you can blame anybody.'

As the strain on his position intensified and demanded more and more time to counter, Flor Crowley also faced a personal dilemma, feeling torn between family and party. Dan Joe O'Mahony feels that ultimately, 'He had to choose between the two. He was very conscious of the fact that he had six kids growing up and he needed to be with them and he did maintain, unless he was with the family, he could not steer them on the right road.'

When the Fine Gael-Labour party coalition called an election in 1977, Joe Walsh was selected to run as a Fianna Fáil candidate, along with Flor Crowley and Vivian O'Callaghan. With their father's seat under threat, the entire Crowley family gathered for the fray. Every room in the house was given over to supporters. At night, party workers gathered in the kitchen, devouring sandwiches and drinking tea, and swopping stories and information on the day's campaigning. The house was like a railway station. Even the household's one non-political animal, Mrs O'Callaghan, became caught up in the frenzy.

'It was like a hive of bees, trying to get here, there and everywhere. The tension up to elections was electrifying. We were all on tenterhooks. Did we do this and did we do that? Who called and who didn't call? There used to be sheets and sheets of paper on the table. We used to have writer's cramp from taking messages.'

When his father went out to face the electorate, thirteen-year-old Brian went with him. He listened to him delivering speeches after Sunday mass in the small parishes of West Cork. He tagged along on the house-to-house canvass in the summer sunshine. At home, he pitched in with his brothers and sisters, running errands and folding leaflets. On voting day he was sent off with rounds of sandwiches to deliver to his father's supporters at the polling stations.

Fianna Fáil won a resounding victory on that day, but the party did so without Flor Crowley. His sister, Kathleen Doyle, who ran the campaign in the Kinsale end of the constituency, recalled the disappointment of losing the seat. 'Nine times out of ten, it's not your opponents you are fighting but your own party, because, I suppose, this is what proportional representation gives you. It gives you that internecine war, that in-fighting.... Politics is a very dirty game, a filthy game, really. It's not something for the faint-hearted. I think you learn as you go along, the hurt that it can bring into your home.'

The Crowleys were stung when Flor's running mate, Joe Walsh, took their father's seat. The loss of the seat was the equivalent of redundancy for Flor Crowley, though the blow was softened by the income from the auctioneering business he had started up after he was first elected.

Shortly after his defeat, Flor was selected to run for the Senate on the Cultural and Educational Panel. When it came to going to Dublin for the Senate election count, Brian went with him. The count is a long, tedious business, and older hands pace themselves as the votes are checked and tallied, but Brian ran between the tables all day, rushing back to tell his father how many votes had been added to his tally when a box was counted. When the vote swung in his father's favour, Brian's face would light up with excitement; he could sense how important this was. Late that night when the result was announced, Flor was elected, and the following morning they drove home, Brian, his aunt and his cousin, and a very tired Flor Crowley. Brian, though, sang all the way to Bandon, from the gates of Leinster House to the back door at Craigie.

Chapter Two

BRIAN SAT IN the darkness of the Pavilion Cinema, tears streaming down his face. He had gone into Cork with friends to celebrate the Inter Cert results, and invested some of the £3 his father had given him on a packet of cigarettes. The smoke made his eyes water and his chest choke, but he kept on puffing all the same. Three or four months after he bought his first pack he was a regular smoker, joining his school friends behind a row of trees in the school field to have a cigarette during break.

His parents had been pleased with his exam results – honours in maths, Irish, English, French, history and geography, and passes in science, accountancy and mechanical drawing – but Brian was far from being a swot. 'I can honestly look back on my schooldays as the best days of my life because of all the friends and the *craic* I had.'

Brian looked more than his age. At fifteen, he was the tallest of the family, big and chunky. He was a fanatical Glasgow Celtic supporter and played soccer on the street and in the field at the back of the house, where World Cups were won and lost by teams with names like 'The Hill of Terror'. His father was very friendly with Fran Fields, who later became chairman of the FAI, and when he got Kenny Dalglish's autograph for Brian, it went up on the bedroom wall beside a huge poster of Debby Harry.

Brian shared a bedroom with his young brother, Flor. His sisters, Fiona and Deirdre, shared a bedroom at the back of the house. As the eldest, Niall and Maeve had the privilege of a bedroom each. They were the natural bosses in the hierarchy, while Fiona, being the youngest was the pet. Flor was the wildest of the boys, always in trouble and always being chastised for his pains. Niall, the eldest, tended to abide by the rules, or at least was careful enough not to get caught when he broke them. Brian got up to more devilment outside.

He loved cars. His father taught him how to start the car and put it in gear, and at thirteen he was out practising in the back field. He was even more enthusiastic about the Scouts. He liked being outdoors, the marching and the weekends away. When they went camping in Kerry, they were flooded out of their field, the rain pouring down on sodden tents and everything in their rucksacks drenched, but no amount of persuasion by his mother and sisters, who had come down to visit him, would bring Brian home with them. Though domestication didn't rate on his teenage agenda, he would spend ages scrubbing a burned-out billycan at the kitchen sink. He enjoyed the parading and the ceremonial activity, taking part in a jamboree in Cappoquin, or forming part of a guard of honour when his father's constituency office and auctioneering office was officially opened by Jack Lynch. On St Patrick's Day the Scouts always lined the sanctuary of the church in Bandon, and when Mrs O'Callaghan came up to the altar rails for communion, Brian would peek out from behind the banner he was guarding and give her a big wink.

Mindful of his reversal in the general election, Flor Crowley opened a pub in Bandon's South Main Street in 1979 when he was a member of the Senate. The pub, known simply as Flor Crowley's, had a big lounge which served as a venue for cabaret, country music and ballad sessions four nights a week. All the Crowley children worked in the pub in their spare time. Brian took to the job immediately, serving customers, washing glasses and horsing kegs of beer out from the storeroom. Outgoing by nature, he enjoyed the wisecracking and was never slow to put himself forward in a group. When Flor Senior put up a trophy for a soccer league, Brian wanted to be in all the photos. He had no inhibitions about it at all; he just leapt in.

The bar opened up a whole new world of people to him, many with lifestyles very different from the temperate behaviour encouraged in the big house up on the Dunmanway Road. Brian enjoyed the buzz. He watched young couples, dressed in their best and out to impress, and puzzled over the broken lives of men who sought oblivion in the bottom of a pint glass.

Helping out in the pub gave him a chance to make pocket-money, and at Christmas time he went into Cork city to work for his uncle, Pat Collins, packing boxes of turkeys and going out in the van to deliver them around the city. He enjoyed being in town with money in his pocket, and when the day's deliveries were finished he would tour the record stores, rifling through the records in the racks. He was getting big into heavy metal.

The cycle of the generations was moving forward during these years, the young Crowleys growing taller than their parents, their grandparents moving on. Both grandmothers lived at Craigie for a while before they died, and Brian's godparents, Granny Collins and her son, Uncle Pat, died while he was in his teens. Brian was close to his godparents and seeing them die was difficult for him. He remembers, 'They were very proud in their own way. They didn't want to show they were in need or suffering. They wanted to put a brave face on.'

Brian left St Fintan's and St Patrick's national schools with a love of history, and he read a lot, but he had no illusions at all about his academic performance at his next school, Hamilton High School. 'I was a very bad student. In reality I was a dosser.'

It's a view that school principal Sean Hamilton is inclined to agree with. As to Brian's confession that he was a dosser, he remarks: 'He had all the natural inclination that way.'

But Sean Hamilton took a liberal view of education. As a teacher, his primary concern was to instil a spirit of independent thinking in his students. A very religious man with a deep love of the Irish language, he set up his first school in 1940 in a few rooms over a chemist's shop in Bandon. Eighteen years later he bought the old premises occupied by the prestigious Protestant school, Bandon Grammar, which was moving across the river to a new location. Some confusion about the legitimacy of the sale arose when it was discovered that a clause in the title deeds prohibited Papists from owning the building, which had been built as four homes for the gentry. The Protestant Schools Society, which did not support this anachronism, sought legal advice. Sean Hamilton remembers going to meet senior counsel, and later Taoiseach, John A. Costello in the Four Courts with Grammar School Principal Ivan McCutcheon. The barrister's advice was brief. 'In the middle of it, he said, "Unconstitutional. Fifty Guineas," turned on his heel and walked off.'

Old as the building was, Brian found it housed a very modern spirit of education. In first year, new pupils were given the discipline and the ground rules. After that they were treated as young adults by the teachers. There was room for free discussion, on politics or whatever other subject, and if students put forward a different point of view, and put it forward properly, there was no hassle. There was a sense of discipline, and there were teachers who doled out punishment with a leather strap, but there was also a certain freedom which was not apparent in other schools.

In his first year in Hamy's, Brian's English teacher, Paddy Keogh, gave his class Alexander Solzhenitsyn's *One Day in the Life of Ivan Denisovich* to read. They were to read it at their leisure, and there were no questions to answer or examination to face. Brian didn't understand the book, but he could grasp the power of Solzhenitsyn's writing, the immensity of his work, and the stunning contrast he created between the bleak beauty of Siberia and the suffering of the men imprisoned there. The book gave the young student an idea of what could be achieved by language, and gave him a source of inspiration which he would return to again and again.

If he was inspired by the Russian writer, it was not so with poetry, which he hated, whether it was in Irish or English. On the other hand, his love of history, inspired by the legends of Fionn MacCumhail and the Children of Lir learned in national school, now grew to a fascination. He read of de Valera and the founding of the state, but other than his study of history, he did just enough to get by. He rarely gathered sufficient momentum to tackle his homework until late at night, and if he thought there was any chance his father was going to be late, he would suddenly discover an essay that he had forgotten or extra home-work that had to be done for the following day, so that he would be up when Flor arrived home.

He was very close to his father and spent as much time with him as he could. When Flor became a member of the Council of Europe in the late 1970s, he would always make a point of bringing foreign coins home for Brian, and he brought Brian with him on one of his trips to Paris. They went to see the Republic of Ireland play France in soccer and afterwards they wandered round Paris, enjoying the sights and sounds of the city. When they got back to the hotel, their energy still wasn't spent and they started fooling round the room, wrestling on the bed until suddenly the bed broke under them. Chastened by the sudden collapse, they confessed and paid for the damage.

Later they travelled to Rome on a family holiday. As he stood in the Coliseum, Brian felt he could hear the lions roaring and the people cheering. The city's sense of history came alive for him. In the Forum he tried to imagine a debate amongst the Senators.

Brian was proud of his father's political standing, though in some ways being Flor Crowley's son was a huge constraint. Everybody knew you, or could very quickly place you. Like his brothers and sisters, Brian was conscious of the rules, conscious of the need, as a politician's child, to keep up appearances. 'We were always aware that people knew who we were, so we couldn't be found to do anything wrong. Even if it was only stealing apples, it didn't matter.'

If the Crowleys were conscious of being in the public eye, there was also a private eye trained on them: Mrs O'Callaghan. 'If the Crowleys were told not to do something, they wouldn't do it. Ours would chance it behind our back, but the Crowleys would not because I'd be out around the town and I'd hear what was going on.' Even when there were no reports, she would check on them just the same, saying she had heard such and such a thing 'when I mightn't be after hearing it at all.'

In school, Brian pasted Fianna Fáil stickers on his schoolbooks with the enthusiasm of a teenager for a rock group, and when one of his teachers insisted he take them off, he refused. When the teacher tore them off, Brian came back the following day with new stickers on the books. His talent for argument brought him into school debating team and he found he was good at it. While his friends on the team put a lot of work into writing out their speeches on prompt cards, Brian would often talk off the cuff and take a chance on being all right on the night. He became good friends with another guy on the team, Kieran Coughlan, who had started in Hamy's after his father had moved to Bandon as manager of the AIB. They hung around with Don Whelton and John Whelton, who were cousins, and John O'Regan. They were a mixed bunch, the sons of a trade union official and a bank manager, an electrician, a shopkeeper, and of course a politician. They were 'townies'. Dedicated card-players, they gathered after school to play thirty-five in the chip shop and on Friday nights they went to Brian's house for a rubber. There was a poker school in the house on Thursday nights, but that was reserved for the 'senior division'.

Brian was discovering Eric Clapton and bands like Deep Purple from listening to Kieran's big brother's records, and he began learning to play guitar with Kieran and Don but didn't keep it up. They were listening to Radio Luxembourg and head-banging to heavy metal groups at the local discos. Brian went to his first disco in the corrugated village hall in Kilbrittain after he had done his Inter Cert. He was heavy and felt awkward, and neither he nor his friends had yet faced the terror of asking a girl out, but they were getting there. Every afternoon students from Hamy's, the Convent School and the Vocational School gathered in the square, waiting for buses to take them home. Brian would hang around with the gang before heading up the road to his own house. He liked being in a group.

Brian turned sixteen in March 1980. Heavy and ruddy-faced, he towered over his classmates at a height of six feet two and weighed close on sixteen stone. He was strong as well as being big; the previous summer he had worked as a building labourer for a few weeks in Ballinspittle. His birthday present was to be allowed to go to Paris on a school tour at the end of the month. It was a lark, ducking off out of sight of their teachers, egging each other on to try out their pidgin French on the local girls, half scared yet half hoping that the continental sophisticates would respond. When they got back to school in early April, they faced the prospect – unique to Hamy's – of sitting a second Inter Cert examination in fourth year. It was time to get the books out in a bid to compensate for the evenings spent card-playing and hanging around with the lads.

BRIAN bounded down the old wooden staircase from his bed-room two steps at the time and landed on the tiled hall with a thump of his black leather shoes. He stuck his head round the sitting-room door. Sally was reading the paper and his two cousins, over from England for the Easter holidays with their father, were watching television. 'I'm just going down town to the office to get some notes photocopied,' he told his mother, waving a fist of white sheets in his hand. Sally looked up from the paper and smiled at him. He was wearing a navy fisherman's jumper – the one she liked best on him – with the collar of his check shirt showing above the neckline. 'Don't be late for your tea,' she told him, but he had vanished down the hall to the kitchen where his sister Fiona was sitting at the table. She began to ask him to get her some stamps in town, but he was already heading out the back door.

It was 17 April and the afternoon was dry and bright. With no breeze to disturb them, plumes of smoke rose stiffly from the chimneys of Bandon's terraced three-storey houses. Brian hummed to himself as he walked down the hill towards town. The early spring sunshine gleamed on the fanlights over the doors of Georgian houses on Kilbrogan Hill. He passed the bootjack which stood outside the door of Neville's solicitors and the saddlery beside the stone bridge which dated back to 1773. He caught the weedy tang of the river as he crossed the narrow, metal foot bridge. Mallards and seagulls stood on a mud islet. The sound of the weir carried loudly in the stillness.

'How's the form, Eileen?' he greeted his father's secretary, Eileen Cronin, as he pushed in the door of the office. As she ran through the notes on Shakespeare's *Coriolanus*, Eileen asked him how the French girls had treated him in Paris. 'There's nothing in my head now but Shakespeare,' he told her.

Back out on the street, he took a short cut through Goods' Hardware Shop to reach the riverside laneway which runs behind the smart facades of South Main Street. The AIB building was only ten doors up the street, but he and his friends generally went round the back and climbed up the stairway behind the bank. Kieran Coughlan was in the kitchen with Don and John Whelton when Brian came in. They fell around laughing when they saw he was carrying the Shakespeare notes.

Shakespeare sat on the shelf as they lounged in Kieran's bedroom, chatting about their adventures in Paris. Eventually they grew listless and someone suggested they go out and bash around with the rugby ball. They all played rugby at Bandon Rugby Club at under-16 and minor level, and they often trained together after school. Brian played hurling also, at school and with Bandon GAA Club.

They picked up the ball and went out on to the stairway, and climbed on to a flat, felt-covered roof which ran parallel to the bank building. At the end nearest the bank, there was just a drop of a couple of feet to another roof. At the other end, the drop fell fifteen feet to the yard below. They decided to play a game of tip-rugby, two against two. Brian took up a position at the exposed end and they tipped off.

The ball sped backwards and forwards across the roof as the lads passed it to their partners, skipping around one another, one pair trying to keep the ball, the other trying to snatch it. The game began to warm up. They chased and ran, shouting to one another. Brian ran to take another pass. Stepping back too quickly to catch the ball, his foot caught on a ledge at the side of the roof and he tumbled backwards. In the frozen moments of his falling, he thought he was going to die. Then he slammed on to the ground.

Panic stricken, his friends rushed down the steps. Brian lay on his back, a crimson trickle seeping from his ear. When they saw him they thought he was dead. Then they heard his moaning.

Kieran rushed into the house to call the ambulance and brought a blanket to cover Brian. He was recovering consciousness, struggling feebly, but his friends restrained him. They knew from their rugby training that if someone is injured in a scrum, you don't move him.

The doctor arrived. Brian was awake now, asking the doctor to straighten his legs which he felt were folded under him. But his legs were stretched out straight on the ground. Doctor Michaels took a needle and inserted it in Brian's leg. Brian made no response. His friends stood watching. Afterwards they tried to reassure one another that Brian would be all right, but Kieran knew what the doctor was checking for.

Niall had been working in the bar when he heard Brian had been injured in a fall at the bank. He raced across South Main Street, through the bank and into the yard, and knelt down beside his brother. Brian was mumbling something: 'Please put my feet down out of the air.'

'I will never forget that. We learned later that the sensation of having your feet in the air is quite common. He had his back on the ground and was paralysed from the waist down, so he assumed his feet were in the air.'

When Sally Crowley came into the yard and saw Brian on the ground, she knew straight away that it was very serious. She had been at home when Kieran O'Driscoll ran to the house to tell her that Brian had had an accident. 'He was just lying there. I knew it was life and death. I was praying and praying and praying.' She went over to reassure the other boys, Kieran and Don and John, asking them if they were OK.

The ambulance arrived and Flor Crowley piled into the back as they sped off, siren blaring. He cried all the way to the hospital. His son had always been such a great character, 'full of life and fun, and a good athlete. It was the only bad break I had in my life,' Flor says, 'the only thing I could never cope with.' In the stretcher bed, Brian lay sick and moaning, struggling occasionally against the straps that bound him down.

He came to in the intensive care unit of Cork Regional Hospital. Wires led from his chest to monitors beside the bed. He could hear the sound of the machines. He didn't know if he was dreaming. He pinched his leg and felt nothing. He pinched his arm.

'Just then an intern came in and I said, "Tell me, am I paralysed?"' The young doctor hedged. 'We don't know yet,' he responded. Brian pressed him again for an answer. The doctor told him he was paralysed for now, but that it might not be permanent. When Sally and Flor came into the room a short time later, Brian told them, 'I'm paralysed but I'll be OK.'

He had no comprehension of what paralysis would mean. He didn't consider whether or not he would be in a wheelchair. That came later. Right now he felt that the fact that he wasn't dead meant he was going to be all right.

Sally stayed on in the hospital while Flor went home to Bandon. Through the long night one thought sustained her: Brian wasn't brain-damaged. 'That was the one thing I held on to from the minute he was able to talk to me. In fact he had a fracture at the base of his skull, and in my ignorance I didn't realise this could have a very serious effect. But the fact that Brian was talking to me, that he spoke coherently, was what mattered to me then.'

Relatives and friends came and went all that night and the following day. At such moments, families discover the depths of their resources. Dr Dan Buckley, whose brother was married to Sally's sister, stayed at Sally's side, walking up and down the hospital corridors, 'talking about positive things'. At home in Bandon the family was in shock. When Mrs O'Callaghan turned up for work the following day, Flor and a neighbour, Peggy Brennan, were still sitting in the kitchen. Flor told her that Brian had had a fall and that he would be in a wheelchair as a result. 'Go away. Don't be codding me,' she said, reaching for her cigarettes. It took a week for the reality to sink in.

Fr Pat Crowley and Sally's brother, Gerard Collins, postponed their return to England and divided their time between the hospital and the Crowley home. Fr Pat tried to keep a lid on things, to keep them from falling apart. Flor was a hard-nosed politician who didn't show too much emotion usually, but his brother could not pacify or console him. Brian's father was in turmoil, 'in a desperate state'. After the first night at the Regional Hospital, he couldn't bring himself to see Brian again until he was transferred to Dublin. He could not draw his mind away from the physical consequences of the accident. He didn't think in terms of Brian being paraplegic or disabled; he had no time for those diagnostic phrases. He feared his son would be a cripple.

Chapter Three

AS THE ORDERLIES rushed Brian through the hospital corridors to the waiting helicopter, his mother followed
behind his stretcher-trolly. People had remarked on
how strong she was and how well she was coping, but the calm
exterior concealed what she was feeling inside. 'I was
broken-hearted. People would say Sally's this and she's that – I
wasn't a bit great, but somebody had to keep the show going.'
She felt she had to be positive and firm and put on a brave face,
though every time she arrived at the intensive care unit she
shuddered at the thought of what she would find on the other
side of the door.

Although catscans had established that Brian had suffered no
brain damage as a result of the fracture to his skull, three of his
vertebrae had been crushed in the fall, injuring his spine and
paralysing him from the waist down. He had also suffered a
partial loss of hearing in his right ear. After three days in Cork
Regional it was felt he would have to be brought to the National
Medical Rehabilitation Centre in Dublin, and an Air Corps
helicopter was dispatched to Cork to collect him. It travelled
only a short distance of the route to Dublin when it was decided
to turn back because Brian had begun to bleed from the ear.
They tried again the following day.

When they touched down he was transferred from the
helicopter-ambulance straight to the x-ray section at the centre,

complaining of pain in his abdomen and his head. He was laid in a large rota-rest bed, whose slow rotation helped his breathing and prevented complications of pressure sores and ulcers. An intravenous drip was attached to his body. In his rotating 'cradle' he was helpless as a baby again, dependent on others to look after him. His mother and father sat watching their deathly still son as he was rocked slowly, first away from them, then back, the motion slow, unceasing, irrevocable.

He lay there for a month, the early weeks a time of intense pain. Although when the worst pain had subsided, lying on his back he could read books and newspapers, listen to the radio and talk to visitors, nevertheless he spent long hours alone.

'Unless you had patience in that situation, you would never survive, because you would go totally off your game. There's nothing you can do. No matter how much you might want something, it's not going to be done unless somebody is ready to do it. You just have to wait.' He had never been patient before the accident; if he wanted something, he wanted it quickly. Now he found himself facing an entirely new reality.

Visitors were especially important to help him through those early weeks. His family and the staff at the centre combined to surround the sixteen year old in a positive, supportive environment. His mother stayed in Dublin for three weeks, willing Brian to get better, encouraging and comforting him. His sister, Maeve, who was studying in Dublin, called often and brought some of her college friends with her. There was a constant stream of letters and cards. 'People are so good to you when the chips are down,' Sally Crowley recalls. 'I will never forget them for it.'

Niall found his first visit to the centre daunting, even worse than when he had gone to see his brother in Cork. His first shock was when he saw a man working at reception who seemed to have no body from the waist down. 'Walking through the corridors and wards, you'd wish you were in a tunnel so that you couldn't see right or left, because everyone you saw was in such crisis. I had to find Brian, but at the same time I didn't want to look, because I was so afraid of what I might see.' During his early visits Niall found the sadness 'unreal', but as time went on he began to realise the vibrancy and life which pulsed through the wards, despite the damaged bodies and the broken dreams.

Brian's younger brother, Flor Junior, was twelve years old when the accident happened; he had just made his Confirmation. He and Deirdre came up from Bandon with their parents, and though Flor and Sally had tried to prepare him for how he would find Brian, he was so shocked by the experience that he got physically sick in the ward. Later, he felt Brian's age was a particular advantage in helping him to cope with disability. He was at the right age for an accident to happen, Flor thought, just old enough to have formed friends, and young enough to re-form his life.

When he began to come back to himself, Brian opened a visitor's book and kept it beside his bed. One of its first signatures was Liam Cosgrave's, the former Taoiseach and Fine Gael leader. Brian's eyes opened wide when he saw Cosgrave enter the ward, and he continued to call every second week with his wife, Vera. Liam Cosgrave and Flor Crowley shared a passion for horse racing and met regularly at racing meetings, and in politics old friendships can sometimes be as enduring as old rivalries. 'The first time he came in, I was shocked,' Brian said. 'After that it was grand and I looked forward to his visits. It couldn't have been easy for him. He didn't know me and there was a huge age gap and so on.' At other times the ward could have housed Fianna Fáil meetings. Every lunchtime, Flor Crowley came out from the Senate, and Fianna Fáil friends Ray MacSharry and Mark Killilea called regularly.

While Brian suffered the burden of his injuries, his friends were shocked emotionally, and found it very hard, as one said, 'to accept really that it should happen to a tower of a young fellow like that'. One of Brian's closest friends, Jim O'Driscoll, who had been one of his leaders in the Scouts, came as far as Dublin to see him, but daunted by the thought of what lay ahead, turned around and went home again. Kieran Coughlan and the Whelton cousins, who had been on the roof with Brian, experienced the same trembling in July when they came to see Brian for the first time since the accident. On the train up with John O'Regan and John Crowley, they wondered what to expect, anxious that they wouldn't know what to say or that their friend would now be very different. It was the day of the Wimbledon final, so they gathered round a television to watch Bjorg and McEnroe on centre court. Brian was being Brian, cheerful and chatty. When they asked him about his injuries, he pointed out the quadriplegics in the room and said he was lucky not to be as badly disabled as they were. What was going on in his mind and what he thought when his friends weren't there, they didn't know, but they felt relieved that he was still the same guy.

And as so often happens, the patient gave huge support to the people concerned about him. 'He was there with his smiley face,' Sally remembers. 'He was just an example. I said, if he can cope with it, it's time everyone else got on with coping with it in a proper fashion.'

In the slow weeks that the cracks in his bones were beginning to heal, the sixteen year old was also beginning to adjust to a new type of life. 'The thought process of coming to terms with it happened over a relatively short period. I realised that's the way it is and that's the way it's going to be. At the same time, I don't think I was ever fully aware of what was going to be involved. I never hoped to walk again. I hoped or prayed that I would be able to handle it, to be able to live with it.'

All around him he could see others learning to live with disability, and coping with what had been a sudden, traumatising change in their lives: Bernard Healy, a nineteen-year-old from

Skerries, who had been injured playing rugby; Michael Chambers, a Clare man in his thirties, hurt in a car accident; Declan Burke from Tipperary and Colm Whooley from Dublin, young men in their early twenties injured in motor-bike accidents. There were young children, one of whom died while Brian was there. 'There were people around who were much worse than I was. They were paralysed from the neck down, or couldn't move their hands, or had to be fed all the time. Though I was lying on the flat of my back for three months, I could see that I could do a lot more even at that stage than many of the people around me. There was a natural taking heart for yourself that you were that much better, that things could have been worse.'

The impact of losing his physical mobility was enormous. Brian felt at a loss at the thought of never again being able to walk or run, to dance or play football. He steeled himself not to dwell on what was missing. He didn't allow himself to think of what he would not be able to do because he was paralysed. And to a certain degree, he was spared the full comprehension of how disability would affect his future by a measure of innocence on his part. He concentrated on the tasks immediately to hand and pushed himself physically to get as mobile as he possibly could.

He was often frustrated by the apparent slowness of his progress through the first two and a half months that he lay in hospital. Recurrent kidney infections, which were to continue for nearly three years after the accident, were a nightmare. The infections, which resulted primarily from the shock sudden paralysis caused to his system, were compounded by the prolonged period lying immobile in bed. He came to fear them. The attack began with a headache, and a sense of foreboding in the pit of his stomach. He began to grow pale and his feet started to swell. He knew it was beginning. His temperature rose until his body was shaking uncontrollably, the bed shuddering as the convulsions gripped his body. Then the searing heat fell away until an ice-like cold seemed to penetrate his bones. He shivered and clenched his teeth to stop them from chattering. It took nine to ten hours, sometimes a whole day, and massive doses of antibiotics before the terrors abated. 'If I ever had the feeling, "Why me?" it would have been at that time. You could feel it coming on the day before and you knew there was nothing you could do only go through with it when it came.'

As the kidney infections wracked his body and sent his temperature soaring and falling, his mood often mirrored his physical well-being, swinging from high to low and then back again. When he suffered infections his spirits dropped at the setback, another delay to his progress. There was nothing he could do about it. He could only lie there, keeping up his hopes, until such time as his body regularised itself.

APRIL passed and took with it the excruciating pain that had characterised his first few weeks in hospital. In May, as the cherry blossom began to bloom in the avenues around Dun Laoghaire, Brian grew impatient with his continuing confinement. In June the back of his bed was raised by the gentlest of degrees, so that his head was tilted upwards and the unrelenting view of the ceiling gave way to a fuller vision of the ward. Eventually he was sitting up in bed, or rather, learning to sit up. It was a weird experience. Having spent three months lying horizontally, his balance was entirely out of kilter. Sitting in bed he felt he was going to fall. He gripped the edge of the bed, feeling a kind of vertigo, afraid he was going to tip over on to the floor. It took him about a month to get his balance right, two weeks sitting in the bed and two weeks sitting in the wheelchair.

Getting the wheelchair was a milestone. It was an antique, a big cumbersome model, built like a tank and very difficult to move. When he made his first attempt to get into the chair, he found it was more difficult than it looked. He pulled himself into a sitting position on the edge of the bed, holding on to the bed with one arm and gripping the arm-rest of the chair with the other. Now he had to lift himself off the bed, swing his hips into the chair and then physically lift his legs on to the footplate. Like the cyclist Sean Kelly, who attributed his success to staying on the bike, for the wheelchair user it's a matter of staying in the chair. He fell out a few times at first. Because his arm muscles were not strong enough to take his weight, his arms were in bits with pain for the first couple of weeks from using muscles which had never had to do anything like this before.

Though the wheelchair might have seemed to symbolise his confinement, it meant freedom to Brian after three months in bed, freedom to move to another stage and another progression along the path that would eventually lead him out through the front door of the hospital.

In the physiotherapy centre, the smell was of sweat and rubber exercise mats. The voice of the physiotherapist and groans of exertion carried through the big, hollow room: 'Come on Brian, you're doing fine. Just a few more inches and we'll call it a day!' His knuckles were white, his arms shaking under the weight of his body as he gripped the parallel bars. Frowning with concentration, he willed his stomach muscles to shunt the dead weight of his calipered legs. The object of the exercise was to encourage the circulation of his blood; the effort was excruciating. The hospital porters used to joke with Brian about his weight when they got to know him. The day he arrived by helicopter, they had gone out to stretcher in the young fellow from Cork, and to their dismay they had to struggle under the weight of a sixteen year old who weighed over sixteen stone. Recurrent kidney infections had melted three stone away. Now, his face was leaner, older.

Every morning from nine until noon, there was intensive training in the physiotherapy centre. To strengthen his arms and tone up muscles which had grown lax after months of inactivity in bed, Brian trained with weights, measuring his progress by the increase in the amount he was able to lift. 'I think the rebellion in me, against the accident and against the disability, was channelled through the physical exercise of getting fitter, getting better and being able to do things. That was my way of getting rid of my aggression.'

In the afternoons there was occupational therapy and training in personal skills, such as learning to get in and out of bed, to get on and off the toilet, to dress and undress. 'Literally, it's like being a child, learning to crawl and to walk, learning how to tie your shoelaces. It's a new way of doing things. It is a whole retraining process, whether it's learning to dress yourself or toilet training.' Learning to dress himself in bed was one of the most difficult tasks; even putting on his socks was a big job. They were also taught practical skills, such as how to cook and to use a computer. 'I enjoyed the welding – it was manly,' Brian quips. One of the most sobering lessons was also the most simple. He had to learn to approach the world around him from the position of someone sitting in a chair, and had to adapt his stance, his movements, his whole perspective to suit. Brian was tall and had always been used to 'looking down' at people. Now the roles were reversed. It didn't play on his mind too much, but at times he would have loved people to appreciate his size – not so that he would dominate, but so people would realise how tall he really was.

But there was little time for brooding at the centre. The staff kept the pressure up, making sure the patients got to their physiotherapy and occupational therapy, even though they might have preferred to have a lie-in. 'That was never allowed. You had to get out and do it. It was brilliant that they did because that gave you the tools to be able to live your own life yourself. I loved it when I was training and when I was doing physical exercises every day. Every day that I was doing physical exercises, it was giving me more power over myself and what I had to do, which meant then that it gave me more independence to go out and do other things. The ultimate goal was to get out of there.'

The Rehabilitation Centre staff, the nurses, doctors, the physiotherapists and occupational therapists, right through to the orderlies who lifted Brian from place to place, gave one the feeling that things were moving forward. They brought a sense of ordinariness to the whole process and created an atmosphere of tremendous comradeship and caring. Waiting for Brian when he first arrived in Dublin had been Aileen McCarthy, who had grown up just a stone's throw from Flor Crowley's old home in Cork. Aileen, whose family were part of Cork's solid business community, had once played golf for Ireland; then, changing the direction of her life, she joined the Mercy Order. 'I never wanted to be a nun as such,' she said. 'I just wanted to be a more useful person than I was.'

After she had finished her training as a nurse, Sr Marie – the name she took in religion – worked at the Mater Hospital and was later assigned to the newly formed Rehabilitation Centre in Dun Laoghaire. She and a group of other nurses, together with a doctor and physiotherapist, were sent to Stoke Mandeville Hospital in England where Sir Ludwig Guttman had pioneered a comprehensive approach to the treatment and rehabilitation of spinal injuries. On their return, they formed the nucleus of the team which ran the national spinal injuries unit at the Rehabilitation Centre.

A woman with a no-nonsense attitude and a wry sense of humour, Sr Marie was one of the driving forces in Brian's rehabilitation. Her philosophy was to encourage people to be independent, to think for themselves and to ask questions about the treatment they received; it concerned their bodies and their lives after all. 'She was the boss,' Brian recalled. 'She was a great motivator and she took no bullshit.' For her part, Sr Marie summed Brian up as 'a young fellow that got on with it. He didn't cry over it. He rehabilitated very quickly.'

He took to heart the message at the core of Sr Marie's philosophy. 'The great thing about my situation was that it was something that I could handle myself. Nobody else could do it for me. Nobody else had an influence on it except me. So the way I turned out, the end result after my rehabilitation, the kind of person I would be, that was up to me, nobody else.'

It became difficult then to decide when to press ahead on his own and when to accept the support which was being offered from all sides, and this created tensions as he became more mobile. Worries about how the accident would affect his family, how his parents and friends would cope, kept nagging him. He didn't want them to feel they had to do anything extra or special for him. He had never seen himself as a dependent.

Being very focused on what he had to do, Brian tried too much to do it all on his own. His belief that he could do it all himself, that he didn't need anyone's help, was not a true reading of the situation, but he only realised this later. 'If you didn't have the support, you wouldn't have been able to do it as well as it turned out. Despite the fact that you may spurn help or assistance, that you may have felt totally independent, because the support was there, you were actually drawing on it even when you may have thought you weren't using it.'

Yet as his range of activity increased so did his desire to be independent of his family. At times, he felt that all their care was smothering. He cut them off sometimes so that he could get on with his rehabilitation. He was conscious too of the pressure which constant visiting must have put on his parents. 'A lot of the time, realising the strain on Mum and Dad coming up every weekend or every second weekend, I'd say, "Don't bother coming to visit me." They would be hurt, but I didn't mean it like that. I just wanted to get it over and done with, to get home as quickly as possible.'

Sally Crowley understood her son's ambition, but she felt that the family allowed him the space he wanted. Brian was, after all, one of six children, so his parents attentions were naturally divided and, she felt, did not focus over much on Brian. When she had seen him in a wheelchair for the first time, she was shocked, but delighted with the advances he was making. 'It was going forward, it showed he was going to be coming home.'

Her instinct that things were 'going forward' was confirmed shortly afterwards, when Brian rang home complaining that Sr Marie wouldn't let him go down to the pub with the others. Sally told Sr Marie that she had no objections, and soon he was off on a new social life in Dublin.

As the summer passed, he became more proficient with the wheelchair and began to discover new pastimes, including archery and pistol-shooting. A note in one of his medical reports stated that he had almost advanced to national standard in archery. He played snooker, and a member of the Irish Wheelchair Association came in and taught him how to drive. He could see himself making progress, could feel himself getting stronger, more used to using his wheelchair, more able to do things for himself. The more he did, the more he realised he had to do. And as he overcame the physical hurdles of his rehabilitation, he realised that there was a further obstacle which would call on deeper reserves of courage and determination.

THE looks started when they queued to pay for admission. They continued inside, obvious even in the semi-darkness. It was a disco night at the Shamrock Rovers Soccer Club, a night for spotting the talent, having a few drinks, maybe getting off with someone. For most of the young fellows there, the night held nothing more daunting than the possibility that a girl would refuse to dance with them. The situation was a little different for the young men in wheelchairs at the edge of the dance floor. There had been a time when they could have walked up to a girl and asked her out.

'You could sense the reaction. But, on the other hand, there were other people there in wheelchairs as well, a support group that you could fall back on. It would have been more difficult if you had to face it totally on your own.'

Brian and some of the other lads 'went out and did things together because we all got into wheelchairs around the same time. We were going through the same kind of stresses and strains and we were coming across the same difficulties.'

Awkward steps and inaccessible buildings were not the greatest difficulties they confronted. For them, the greatest barriers were those they saw in peoples' eyes. 'Peoples' attitude changes because you are in a wheelchair. Even though you're not a different person – your thoughts, your outlook, your hopes or your desires are the same – people's attitude to you does change. That's the most difficult side of it, rather than having to use a wheelchair all the time.'

It was hard, but moving out into the world again wasn't all a test of endurance. There were good times and *craic* and the life of the city waiting to be discovered. With the wheelchair under him, Brian was able to visit family friends and to go to rugby matches at Lansdowne Road with Niall and schoolmates from home. They went to a football friendly between Ireland and Romania. And every chance he got, he went to hear the new bands which were springing up all over Dublin: bands playing their first gigs, like Rocky de Valera and the Gravediggers in the community centre in Sallynoggin; experimental bands like Gavin Friday and the Virgin Prunes, and Katmandu and In Tua Nua, who played in the Purty Loft in Monkstown. He went to hear Stepaside regularly at the Sportsman Inn in Mount Merrion. He was finding out about a whole new style of music, a totally different scene from the cabaret type country and western which was the standard fare at home. He was open to everything, eager to take it in. In Dublin he got a love for live performances and the rawness of experimental music that settled into a desire to try to get into the music world himself.

'Summer in Dublin' by Bagatelle was in the air everywhere that year. It was the song that characterised those months in the Remedial Clinic for Brian Crowley.

I remember that summer in Dublin,
And the Liffey as it stank like Hell,
And the young people walking on Grafton Street,
Everyone looking so well ...

Take me away from the city,
Lead me to where I can be on my own,
I wanted to see you and now that I have,
I just want to be left alone.
I'll always remember your kind words
And I'll still remember your name,
And I've seen you changing and turning,
And I know that things just won't be the same.

Things were changing and turning for Brian, and the summer in Dublin brought him a first breath of romance, too. It was a huge thrill, like nothing he had experienced before: a glowing sensation, a growing up. It made him feel good. In ordinary circumstances it would have happened anyway; now it became a part of his healing. He went out with a few girls, some of whom had boyfriends at the time, but 'it wasn't serious enough to be deemed two-timing'. Some were student nurses at the centre, others friends of the friends he had made there, all of them older than him, all of it casual and friendly.

There were other thresholds to cross, hard lessons which led to a deeper maturity. Brian's group of friends talked among themselves about coming to terms with being disabled. The reality was dawning; they would never walk again. It wasn't a club where they could hand their membership back. The older ones, who were in relationships, were worried about the impact of their disability on those relationships. They all worried about going home, about coping with people's regarding them as different or set apart. Information and insights were traded, and there were plenty of saving moments of black humour. Turned upside down in one of life's crazy moments, sometimes there was nothing else they could do but laugh at it.

There was no formal counselling at the centre, but informal counselling was ongoing. 'As problems arose, questions were raised and answered, and the next stage was outlined so that you would be prepared for that.' Everybody's disability is different; everybody differs in their reaction to it. 'There is no set course you can do. In particular, with an accident like that, it's something you have to come to terms with yourself first and foremost. I don't think anyone can come to terms with it for you. I don't think anybody can guide you. If you have frustrations and depressions, you have to go through them, there's no way of avoiding that.'

Brian chose to deal with things internally for the most part. He was developing an air of self-sufficiency, a sort of internal composure. He didn't know if dealing with things on his own was a personality trait or a protection mechanism. 'As a protection method, it could be protecting yourself from people feeling that you're weak or protecting other people from things that might hurt them. I know that astrologers say that Pisces are like that, they're private people and dreamers with ideals. I'm a Pisces, though I don't believe all astrologers have to say.

'My own opinion is that it's just a personality trait that I have, that I don't need to go pouring my heart out to people to get a solution. If you can work it out in your own mind, and you can work it out for yourself, you're getting to the real answer. Again, you might not always be able to accept the real answer and you have to look again. I think each of us has that little bit that we hold back.'

The accident matured him very quickly. In the Rehabilitation Centre, they were encouraged to ask questions about their treatment and their condition. Sr Marie and Dr Paddy Murray were very open. 'You could ask them any question and you'd get a direct answer. I was only sixteen. As a teenager, you're not used to getting direct answers to serious questions.' He took a matter-of-fact attitude. That was the situation he was in, that was the way it was going to be, so he was going to have to find out how it worked. As he found out more about what paralysis meant, more questions arose. Finding out about the sexual implications of the paralysis was not high on his list of priorities at first, but as time passed he began to question it more. It was explained, but not fully. It couldn't have been, because everybody is different in the way their disability affects them.

Many people have to work through the trauma of finding themselves suddenly disabled. The people in Sr Marie's care react in different ways to their circumstances. People grieve for their lost abilities. For many there are blockages, difficulties in coping; they get angry and depressed. People with a religious outlook often try bargaining with God. A lot of people go on looking for a cure. 'People tend to have a chip on their shoulder, a lot more so nowadays,' Sr Marie says. 'They have a free will but they are still blaming God for the things that went wrong. I don't think that ever happened to Brian. He was one of the lucky ones.'

Brian's uncle, Fr Pat Crowley, was also surprised at how positive Brian was. 'He was saved by not having to deal with bitterness. He never seemed to regard himself as having a disability, so he overcame one thing after the other.'

Religion had always been present in Brian's life; after the accident, it grew increasingly important. He worked out a lot of his attitude to his disability through prayer, lying awake in the quiet hours of the night, talking to God in his own words. 'Psychologically, it was talking to somebody and working it out in your own mind as well.' He recited formal prayers, too, to Mary. He never prayed to be able to walk again, to be cured. He prayed to be able to accept what had happened to him and to cope with it, and he prayed that his mother and father would be able to cope with it as well. Prayer became a part of his rehabilitation process. As a result of the accident, his faith was heightened and personalised, and religion became more intimate when he discovered that he could pray privately and 'have a chat' with God. His belief was strengthened by the fact that he had survived the accident. 'My opinion is that I wasn't meant to die because God or a higher power decided that I wasn't going to. That was a strength and a comfort to me then. From that I developed a deeper faith and belief, giving me full confidence that whatever I do will turn out all right.'

He had to struggle with the question of why he should have been the one to be hurt. Resolving that took some time, but he found a way of understanding it eventually.

'A lot of it is free will. I needn't have gone on the roof. Should God have struck me down before I got on the roof because I was going to fall off?

'The belief I have is that the things that happened, happened because of human nature, because of personal action, not because of a lack of intervention by God or a higher power. In my opinion if there was a miracle, the miracle was that I was able to accept it. That to me was the biggest intervention: that I was able to cope with it and able to accept it.'

Coming so close to death was to have a lasting impact on his approach to life. He had had a hard lesson in the frailty and uncertainty of life, and he was determined to appreciate it more in the future. 'Every day that you're alive is a great thing, simply because you could be dead tonight. I think this gives you a great appreciation of what you have, however minimal or maximum that is. The simple things and smaller things are all welcome.'

He had changed. Since the accident in Bandon in early spring, the chubby, carefree schoolboy had grown into a leaner, more serious young man. By now the autumn leaves were falling, and it was time to take another step.

Chapter Four

S ALLY CROWLEY SAT inside the big plate glass windows of the airport terminal with her daughter, Deirdre, listening to arrivals and departures being announced over the public address system. The Dublin flight had been delayed. Crowds began to gather as planes flew in from other destinations; it was the October bank holiday weekend and Cork Airport was alive with people arriving for the Jazz Festival. As the hands of Sally's watch dragged towards midnight, there was still no sign of the plane. A lifetime ago, she had watched the same sky while a helicopter taking her son away disappeared into the distance. Now he was coming home.

Brian had asked to come down by plane for this, his first weekend home from hospital. His parents splashed out for the occasion, feeling that it would take some of the sting out of being in a wheelchair for Brian. At Dublin Airport, he crossed the air bridge to the plane in his own chair and transferred to a smaller one when he had boarded. When they reached Cork he was taken from the plane by a hydraulic lift which lowered him onto the ground, then he wheeled himself across the tarmac.

In the early, dark days, they had envisaged him coming home on a stretcher, hooked up to equipment and in the care of a nurse. 'I never doubted his spirit for a moment, but at the start I thought he wouldn't be able to do anything physically,' his father said. 'We were wondering how different it was going to be from the hospital where he had people to do things for him the whole time. I didn't realise he would be as independent as he was.'

Patients at the Rehabilitation Centre often had to delay returning to their homes because of the alterations needed to accommodate a wheelchair; some even had to move to new houses. Fortunately, Craigie was an old building with doors wide enough to allow easy passage for a wheelchair, and work was already underway on an extension specially for Brian. For the present a bed was put into the front room for him. Niall would sleep there too to keep an eye on him during the night.

From the very first instant, the family were determined not to treat Brian differently. Their GP had told them that they should just behave like they always had and warned them not to treat him as an invalid. As Brian wheeled himself up the path outside the house, Mrs O'Callaghan opened the front door.

'I always knew you'd get out of your Leaving,' she greeted him, 'but I never thought you'd go so far.'

'That kind of broke the ice for us,' she recalled later.

If the Rehabilitation Centre had been teaching Brian independent living skills, his family ensured that he was not going to be deprived of the opportunity to practise them at home. All that weekend, if he asked one of his brothers or sisters to get something for him, he was told to get it himself. Yet it was a different house now that Brian was back. The trauma of his accident had been hard on all of them. 'It was like a house that was dead,' in Mrs O'Callaghan's words. 'There was nothing said, but they were going around always thinking about Brian.' It was a huge relief to have him home again, though things didn't fully return to normal until they got used to Brian 'in the new way'.

The following morning, Brian set off down town with Don Whelton and Kieran Coughlan. Watching them go out the gate, Sally thought to herself that they would kill him going down the steps on the hill, but she left them go. The process of letting go had begun a long time before, but when she saw Brian now she could sense how much he had changed and how futile it would be to try to stop him.

Brian returned to Dublin on Sunday to continue his rehabilitation. The next few months were difficult for him; he felt that he was well enough to be home and he was anxious to go. He was finally discharged just before Christmas, a little earlier than Sr Marie would have liked.

Returning to Craigie was like when he was a child coming back from summer holidays in Youghal and the whole house would seem to have changed. His brothers brought him upstairs to see his old bedroom; it still looked the same, but of course it was Flor's now. Brian moved into the front room.

He still needed care. He had to be physically turned during the night, and Niall or Flor would get up to help Sally move him. All through Christmas and the weeks that followed, he continued to be wracked by kidney infections. They left the family feeling helpless, there was so little they could do until an attack ran its course. They piled blankets on him when his temperature dropped and gave him cool baths when it rose again. 'He'd be in bed with his temperature roaring and you'd try and cool him down,' Niall recalls. 'Half an hour later he'd be freezing. You'd change his sheets because he was sweating so much and arrange his pillows to make him comfortable. I don't know how he handled it. He would just go quiet.' At best the infection would burn itself out in a day or two. At worst, Brian became so sick that he could not hold down the water or antibiotics so vital to fight the infection, and had to be hospitalised. On a few occasions, Sally and the older children watched white-faced as the ambulance took him away in the middle of the night. Curiously, the worst attacks seemed to happen when his father was away from home.

Brian and Niall had led quite separate social lives up until this; they were different ages and had different interests. Now they found a new closeness. On Niall's part, the closeness was partly a protectiveness born during the fitful nights he watched over his young brother, or caught the glances of people on the street during their first outings with the wheelchair. For his part, Brian's new maturity brought him closer in outlook to Niall. In that sense, the fall had been a bridge which brought them together.

Niall's feeling for Brian deepened when he saw the gutsy way his brother was coping with being disabled. While he was in Dublin, Brian had decided that he would go back to school and do the Leaving Cert with his own class. He wanted to be with his friends and dreaded the thought of staying back a year and joining a class where everyone was younger than him. In Hamy's, the caretaker built a wooden ramp so that his wheelchair could come up the steps to the school door. He used the ramp for the first few days, but then it disappeared as the boys took over completely and brought him wherever he wanted to go. It was a huge adjustment for his friends to make, to learn when it was right to give a helping hand and when it was more appropriate to stand back, but when he needed help, he asked for it, and if he was too stubborn to ask, they gave it anyway. After a while he developed a knack for being self-sufficient without being too blunt and saying, 'Don't do that for me.'

Because of the ongoing problems with his kidneys, he had to return to Dublin for corrective surgery on his bladder and kidneys at the Meath Hospital, and his school attendance was patchy all through the spring. His condition had improved considerably by the time he came home in May, and the incidence of infection was much reduced, though it was another two years before the problem was fully rectified by an operation at the Mercy Hospital in Cork.

On his return, Brian found the household preparing for a general election which had been called for the following month. That campaign signalled the start of trying times in the Crowley household, which had to bear the burden of three elections in a

period of eighteen months and extra financial pressure conse-
quently.

Journalist Vincent Browne described the years from December
1979 to December 1982 as 'one of the most remarkable periods
in modern Irish history'. There were four changes of Taoiseach
in that time, six different Ministers for Finance and three
changes of government. Irish government 'declined progressively
to a level unprecedented for decades'. During the 1981-82
period in which the three elections were held, Fianna Fáil leader
Charlie Haughey, who had worked assiduously through the '70s
to recover his position in the party, faced successive challenges to
his leadership. When he was in Dublin to see specialists for
treatment in February, Brian went with his father to the party's
fiftieth Árd Fheis, where the embattled leader was expected to
quell opposition and group the party behind him. But events
were again to overtake Haughey. A strange silence settled over
the delegates as news came through of a fire at a disco in the
Taoiseach's own constituency. Forty-eight young people, out to
celebrate St Valentine's night, had lost their lives. The Árd Fheis
was cancelled.

In the early months of the year, political debate on the island
was dominated by the hunger-strikes in the north, as republican
prisoners refused food in protest at the British government's
decision to classify them as criminals rather than political
prisoners. In early April, hunger striker Bobby Sands won a by-
election in Fermanagh–South Tyrone when he was forty-two
days into his fast, and his death on 5 May was followed by a
week of rioting across the north. With his death, the hunger
strike entered a darker and more determined phase, challenging
the progress of Anglo-Irish relations and Charles Haughey's handling of them.

When Haughey finally called an election in May, Flor Crowley,
still a member of the Senate, was blocked as a candidate for the
Dáil at the constituency convention, but subsequently he was

added to the Fianna Fáil ticket by the Taoiseach. Once again feelings ran high in the Fianna Fáil organisation in West Cork, and the campaign in the constituency was characterised by party infighting. Flor Crowley found himself having to foot the bill for his campaign literature, adding substantially to the cost of his election campaign.

Brian saw no reason why being in a wheelchair should keep him off the campaign trail. He would have been campaigning for his father if he had not had an accident and did not think he should stop just because of that. He had a personal point to make as well. He wanted to show people that he was not incompetent, that he wasn't in a coma or on a life support machine. And once they saw him in the flesh, most people accepted him without much difficulty. Whenever there was an air of awkwardness, about his accident and the wheelchair, Brian would joke that at least, unlike his father, he would always have a seat.

Getting wrapped up in politics did not leave him much time for pondering his own situation anyway. Brian canvassed with his father in Clonakilty, the heartland of their party rival, Joe Walsh. On the doorsteps, unemployment was a major concern, and the electorate was not happy with the politicians' handling of a situation that had virtually become a crisis. One of the most emotive issues of the campaign was the deaths of the republican hunger strikers. Sinn Féin put forward a H-Block candidate in West Cork, Sean Kelleher, who shared some of the same support base as Flor Crowley. 'A lot of the people who would have been supporting him would have been personal supporters of my father as well,' Brian believes. 'There was a lot of common interest and comradeship among that group of canvassers and us.'

When the votes were counted, most of Sean Kelleher's votes transferred to Flor Crowley and helped him take the seat. The republican connection had come good on this occasion. After the announcement of Flor Crowley's victory at the count in Clonakilty, a convoy of cars brought party workers back to celebrate in Bandon, where the Crowleys had organised a party in the back of the bar. The party, however, had to be abandoned because of a bomb scare.

After the election, the family went on holidays to Youghal. Brian stayed behind in Bandon. Later, he joined them for a summer break in Dingle, but he wasn't very happy while he was there, and went back to Bandon to be with his friends. It was a summer spent at football and hurling matches, discos and parties in friends' houses, trying to get back into the scene. When he first went to the local disco, braving the initial awkwardness, the crowd automatically moved back to make way for him and made him feel even more conspicuous and uncomfortable. In Dublin, the wheelchair hadn't made as much difference when he went out because he was with other disabled people, but at home people felt clumsy in his presence. Even his friends were nervous of him. He confronted them with the attitude: 'Delighted to see you. I'm getting on with my life. What's happening?' but they wondered if he was trying to minimise the difficulties that being in a wheelchair presented. 'He didn't admit the tough times because that could be seen as a sign of weakness and bring out the "God love us" reaction, which he didn't want.'

The biggest frustration he faced was the tedium and the awkwardness of coping with being so immobilised. Actions that would not have cost him a thought before now had to be carried out with care. He had to be careful transferring from his bed or from a car into the wheelchair because he could not afford to fall and hurt himself. Although he had embraced the Rehabilitation Centre's philosophy of living independently, there was no escaping a certain level of dependency. When it came to negotiating flights of stairs, he needed the help of others. There were things that he missed. 'Being able to dive into the sea and go for a swim and feel the waves crashing against you – it would be nice to be able to do that.' He could still go to the beach for a swim, but with much greater difficulty. 'You just can't say "It's a lovely day" and suddenly strip off and dive in. You have to find a way to get down and get near the beach and have someone pull your chair away. It's not so easy to act on impulse.'

As the summer passed, life slowly began to return to normal. 'The boyhood was gone from him,' Mrs O'Callaghan observed. 'As a youngster of sixteen, you'd expect him to go back a bit, petting and looking for sympathy. He didn't. He came forward in leaps and bounds.' Brian's determination to be treated the same as he had been prior to his accident won through by degrees. The strangeness gradually wore off, the looks disappeared and, eventually, he was back to being one of the boys. He and his friends hung around with some girls from the Convent School in Bandon, and they went to discos and films together. At the beginning of the summer he met Lisa Shean and when they went back to school they began to go out together. It was the real boyfriend/ girlfriend thing; he went to her debs and she to his grads. They went out together for about two years, on and off.

After the summer holidays Brian started back at Hamy's a little later than the others because of yet another kidney infection. On his first day back, the maths teacher, Frank Daly, turned to him. 'Mr Crowley, you can look into Mr Whelton's copy.'

Don Whelton opened his copy obligingly, but the page which was meant to display his homework was empty.

'Do you follow that, Mr Crowley?' Frank Daly asked.

'Yes sir, I do,' Brian replied. 'I follow that fully.' Things were returning to normal.

Brian got a car after he went back to school. He was seventeen. A blue Opel Kadet with automatic transmission and hand controls, he drove it for about eighty miles in the back field to get the hang of it. He circled the field again and again, bouncing over the grassy bumps with young Flor beside him to shout 'Stop!' to test his reactions using hand controls rather than pedals. The wheelchair got him round the town, but getting the car meant freedom. 'After that, things began to settle down and I got back to the normal routine. Prior to that I might have been anxious or frustrated about things, about having to get lifts here or there. The car meant that I could spend more time with my friends because I didn't have to wait for my mother or father to collect me.'

Brian wasn't the only student driving to school, but he was the only one who owned his own car, a fact that made him popular with his friends. He drove the gang to school matches and brought them to discos at night, or sometimes they might head into Cork for the day. One night on the way home from a disco outside Bandon, someone threw stones at the car as he was driving away. He turned and drove back, rolled the window down and challenged some guys who were hanging round. His friends weren't protecting him. 'We didn't spoil the guy,' John Hurley says. 'I sat in the car once while it was bucketing out of the heavens, and Brian had to get out the chair and put it together himself. I got out of the car when he was ready.'

When the extension to the Crowley house was complete, Brian had his own bedroom and bathroom, a space of his own where he could bring friends and do his own thing. There were times when he was out very late and his parents were up waiting for him when he came home, and sometimes he got away with more than a seventeen year old usually would, but Sally still knew where to draw the line. Once when one of Brian's friends was drunk, Sally was adamant that he wasn't going to be in their house in that condition if his own mother didn't know about it. She was strict about it. 'Just because he was in the wheelchair didn't give him any more leeway for that. I should have been more strict – I was conscious of not making him a spoiled brat – but then I always felt the car was the thing that kept him sane.'

The car was pressed into service when Brian's father set out on the campaign trail again in February 1982. Fine Gael and the Labour party had formed a coalition the previous summer, but the sense of political instability continued unabated, and the coalition eventually fell when it tried to formulate a budget. The election results gave neither of the major parties an overall majority, but Fianna Fáil returned to office with the support of independent deputies and the narrowest of margins in the house. Flor Crowley, however, lost the seat he had regained in June. His victory had been short lived.

In the winter Brian went to music classes in the evening with John Hurley, Anthony Desmond and some others. John took Spanish guitar; Brian tried the piano. Though his enthusiasm for the piano didn't last very long, his interest in music and his eye for making a few bob – putting petrol in the car was proving costly – encouraged him and Don Whelton to start their own business, promoting discos and bands and organising dances in the local GAA hall and in other halls and hotels around West Cork. The fledgling company was christened 'Dandruff Promotions' by a few of their friends; one explanation of the title was that they were 'head and shoulders' above all the rest. They organised gigs in Flor Crowley's, too, bringing in ballad singers and popular names like Paddy Reilly. They were making up to £30 a week each when their teenage friends were trying to survive on pocket money.

As the Leaving Certificate examination began to loom, some of the teachers gave Brian individual tuition during free classes to bring him up to speed, but though history remained an abiding passion, he was uninterested in much of the rest of the course. He remembers the exam for the fifth question on the history paper: a topic of your own choosing on which you could write a dissertation. He chose the Dáil debates on the Anglo-Irish Treaty of 1921.

Although his results were not brilliant, he passed the Leaving Cert and had no regrets about sitting the examination with just one year of study behind him. He passed maths, French and Irish, and got honours in history, English and business organisa-

The brothers: Brian and Niall

Brian with his father, Flor, on a fishing trip off Donegal in 1975

Brian on his First Communion Day, 1971

Flor Crowley

The Crowley clan. Standing: Brian, Deirdre, Danjo O'Mahoney, Maeve, Niall, Flor jnr; seated: Flor, Fiona, sally

Galaxy at the Rose of Tralee Festival, 1988

At a gig in Cork: Gerry Lane, Jim Dwyer, Brian, Noel Curran

Victory in the European elections (Patrick Casey)

*The Crowley team checking tallies: Dr. Kevin James, Manus O'Callaghan,
Niall Crowley, Kevin Fitzgerald, Humphrey Murphy*

Speaking in the European Parliament

Brian with Ray MacSharry and Charles Haughey

Brian is president of Jack Charlton's Disabled Fisherman's Association

*With NY State Assembly member Joe Crowley (cousin) and Governor
Mario Cuomo, 1994*

Brian Crowley (Barry Murphy)

tion. His teachers had advised him to wait another year before taking the exam, but he refused to be persuaded; he wanted to finish school. He had no interest either in joining the student princes at University College Cork.

What he wanted to do was to go out and make a living, to show that he could hold down a job. Niall tried to persuade him to study law or accountancy – Niall was in UCC studying commerce – but he didn't want to know about it. His parents disagreed with what he was doing, but didn't press him. 'They let me go working in the business down town, in the pub and the auctioneers, but if I hadn't had my accident, I would have been more or less forced to go to college,' he thinks. Sally and Flor would certainly have preferred to see him continue his education, but felt there were other things to be taken into account. 'We knew in our hearts and souls that there were more important things than what he got in his Leaving Cert. You had to weigh up whether to push him and make him go to college or let him go out and work. He had coped so well with all the adjustments. Flor and myself felt that, having spoken to him, that just to get a BA wasn't the most important thing. We felt that what he did was right. He might have done nothing in college. He might have just been one of the lads, flitting around in his car and his wheelchair.'

Their school days over, many of Brian's friends turned their faces to distant horizons while he stayed behind in Bandon, intent on carving out his future at home. They decided to set down a marker for their parting of the ways. Hoping to ensure that they would all meet up at least once a year, they put together a fund to buy a trophy for a poker tournament which they would play every Christmas.

Chapter Five

AFTER HE LEFT school, Brian went to work in his father's auctioneering firm. He began to do valuation work for solicitors and to handle sales of houses and farms, learning the trade from other auctioneers, building up experience as he went along. Previously, the firm had been run by employees of his father's but Brian was now the only one running the office, and he went out looking for business. The big trend in property was the number of bungalows coming on the market, but around Bandon buying, selling and leasing farmland was still the mainstay.

One time, as Brian pored over the map of a farm, he was intrigued by the series of crosses marked among the outline of the fields. The map had been handed into Flor Crowley's auctioneering office by a firm of solicitors to do a valuation for probate. At first Brian thought the marks might indicate the presence of wells or springs, but there seemed to be too many of them. When he went out to check the land, he knew for certain that the crosses had nothing to do with water.

On his next trip, Brian brought a man with him to dig around the areas indicated on the map. At the place marked by the first cross, he shovelled away the sods and earth until, about a foot and a half below the surface, he uncovered an old tin box. When they opened it they discovered it was stuffed with old fifty and one hundred pound notes, seven or eight hundred pounds in all.

There were about ten marks on the map, and each site yielded a similar treasure. In the end, they recovered enough to save the farmer's widow from having to sell the farm.

Bandon also had a big hunt, with training and breeding horses big business in the surrounding area, so he went into association with a Wicklow man to hold saddlery auctions in Bandon twice a year. As he didn't know enough about horses or horses' equipment, he brought in another local auctioneer to handle the auction itself; Brian was the contact, taking care of the organising and the paperwork, and splitting the fees between the principals. Initially, he subcontracted the actual auctioning of land and property, but after a while he began to hold the auctions himself.

The wheelchair was a hindrance, of course. There were obvious difficulties; access to buildings was usually a problem, and he couldn't go upstairs with clients to show them right through premises. People who knew him only through speaking to him on the phone were often taken aback when they discovered he was disabled, though when they saw how he was operating, and as he himself became more practised, the wheelchair became less of an issue or an obstacle.

Auctioneering gave Brian a grounding in business and in dealing with people. He learned about keeping his affairs to himself, as clients interested in buying property were never anxious for others to know their business or the money they were paying, and he picked up one other valuable insight – how difficult it was to get money from people. If a property was advertised and didn't sell, clients were loath to part with cash to pay for the promotion. It was frustrating work at times, but when it came right he got a huge thrill out of putting together the elements of a sale: finding the purchaser, fixing the price, arranging the finance – in short, making the deal.

In Dublin, a deal of a different kind was beginning to come unstuck. The Taoiseach, Charles Haughey, faced into the eye of another storm in October as dissatisfaction with his leadership was fuelled by a series of embarrassments to the government. This was the year of GUBU, an acronym invented by Conor Cruise O'Brien from Haughey's description of the sequence of events which wounded his administration as 'grotesque, unbelievable, bizarre and unprecedented'. In November, Haughey lost a vote of confidence in Leinster House. The ensuing general election, on 24 November, ushered in a Fine Gael–Labour coalition which instigated the 'liberal crusade' which was to dominate political debate through the 1980s. It was Flor Crowley's last tilt at regaining the West Cork constituency. He lost again to Joe Walsh in what the *Magill Book of Irish Politics* described as a 'bitter battle'.

Two months later, during the Senate election campaign in January 1983, Flor Crowley suffered two heart attacks and was hospitalised as a result. He was advised to retire from politics. Looking back on this traumatic end to eighteen years in politics, Flor Crowley expresses nothing but relief. 'It was a great release to be told by the doctor to give up politics because my heart was not in good condition. It was like lifting a huge boulder off my back. I was delighted with the news. That may sound perverse, but I no longer had the responsibility of going fighting this thing in politics. I could legitimately withdraw from it with a clear conscience. I was forty-eight.' Despite retiring when he did, he suffered another heart attack the following year. 'He would have been dead if he had stayed in politics,' Brian believes. 'It was a blessing in disguise for him. Everybody was relieved it was over.'

Brian had been giving a hand in the Crowleys' pub, buying stock, supervising cash and dealing with suppliers. He still dabbled in music promotion, bringing musicians like contemporary singer–songwriter Freddie White to play in the bar. But the roller-coaster ride through eighteen months of electioneering had drained more than just energy from the Crowley household. While Flor Crowley poured his resources into fighting three elections in a row, the Crowley family's business had been neglected and, financially, the family was sailing close to the wind. Each election campaign had cost dearly. The combined total of all three came close to £30,000. In 1983 the bar was taken over by a liquidator, who ran it, still under the name Flor Crowley's, until it was sold.

The Crowleys were facing into lean times, but Brian and his teenage friends were still unstinting in their enjoyment of the *craic*, socialising in the pubs around Bandon and Clonakilty, going to dances and discos, heading off to summer festivals. Brian's car gave them mobility. They might be in a pub in Bandon at closing time and one of the lads would say, 'There's a disco in Skib,' and they would pile into the car and head for Skibbereen. They thought up stories to explain how Brian had ended up in a wheelchair, each one more far-fetched than the next. A particular favourite was that Brian was a singer who had been hurt in an accident, whose wife and two kids had left him afterwards. One night when they were out, Brian had two chairs, and one of his friends got into the second one... A miracle was witnessed in West Cork that night.

Brian's school friend Barry Slattery had moved to Castleisland, but they met up regularly, going on the town in Cork city or heading off to small West Cork villages in the summer. And wherever Brian went, there was usually no shortage of girls, a set of circumstances his friends weren't slow to capitalise on. 'I suppose he would be described as good-looking, maybe the long hair, I don't know, but certainly he always got on with them. Your chances of picking up a girl were always much better if he was around.'

When he went to rent a premises in Bandon to Dave Heffernan, and discovered he was using it to set up a pirate radio station, Brian immediately offered to present a show. He was soon doing a regular slot on WKLR, from midnight until 3 am, four nights a week. Influenced by international stations such as the ship-based Radio Caroline, pirate stations were springing up all over the country; Nova and Sunshine had taken to the airwaves in Dublin while Cork city had its own South Coast Radio. The pirates' buccaneer image was greatly enhanced when raids by the Department of Post and Telegraphs were widely publicised, though many of the 'pirate' DJs eventually entered mainstream broadcasting on board RTE's new station, 2FM.

Brian wanted to produce an alternative to the commercial pop music which dominated the new stations. He steered clear of chart hits, concentrating instead on Irish bands and traditional groups, and raiding his father's classical collection to add another dimension to his eclectic selection. His friends often dropped in to keep him company on the graveyard shift. While Barry Slattery went to put on the kettle, Brian introduced the discs, and John Hurley cleared a space on the cluttered table for bags of burgers and chips: the late nights made Brian ravenous. Between songs, they joked and talked and drank endless cups of coffee. Into the early hours of the morning, and Brian played comedy selections and invited listeners to phone in their choices of music. He also introduced a telephone link with West Cork people living in Dublin. Zapping from comedy to classical, local chat to lonesome airs, he signed on and off the airwaves under the sobriquet 'Brian Rogers and the 25th Century', which resulted in him being nicknamed Buck for a long time afterwards.

But at home, the fact that the Crowley household was under some strain was apparent to the young Crowleys as much as to their parents. 'As an adolescent,' Niall recounts, 'you had this sense of "Are we going to survive; are we going to hold on to the house?" We had a relatively trouble-free childhood and then things just went bang, bang, and we suffered two major blows.' The auctioneering office closed. 'When my father's business went under, he made the headlines because he was a politician,' Niall Crowley says. 'There were times we had to trim the cloth at home. In a funny kind of a way, a lot of us inherited my mother's quality of cutting your cloth according to your measure; she's a cautious woman. We're not that much into material things, but none of us ever want to experience that type of defeat in politics again, or the business going down the tubes.'

When his father's business closed, Brian continued to do some freelance auctioneering work, and he tried a new venture, going on the road selling stationery for a printing company. It was the hardest job he had ever done: ninety-nine per cent of the businesses he called to had all the letterheads and billheads they needed. It was time to try something different.

FROM the vantage point of the stage, the concrete hall with its sky-high roof is like a big, empty football pitch. Rock music is rolling around the hollow space and spilling out into the car park with the light. Young fellows, sleeves rolled up and hands in pockets, drift in on a cloud of aftershave, awkward despite their determined air of nonchalance. In the Ladies the harsh light is merciless. A line of girls with arms folded queue for the cubicles while others exchange make-up at the mirror and rearrange their freshly shampooed hair. It's the October Bank Holiday Weekend and Galaxy is playing at a Macra na Feirme dance. Three musicians are tuning up and the third one, the guy with the long hair in the wheelchair, he's supposed to be a brilliant singer.

At quarter to twelve, the crowd is bunched in one corner of the hall while a small group in leather jackets bounce around in front of the stage, head-banging to the heavy metal. Behind them is an open expanse of space and no amount of heavy rock is going to lure the rest of the crowd into it.

'We're up shit creek on this one,' Brian tells the others. They consider a change of tactics.

They know about five waltzes between them. As they ease the

tempo gently into 'The Lonely Woods of Upton' and 'It's a Long, Long Way From Clare to Here', couples begin to venture into the great abyss, but the band's repertoire of waltzes is soon exhausted and desperate measures are needed to keep the momentum going. They take numbers like Status Quo's 'Rocking All Over the World' and AC/DC's 'A Whole Lot of Rosie' and convert them to three/four time. The rock-blues band looks as if it's got a Strauss ball on its strings in the middle of rural Cork.

A similar scenario is repeated on Sunday night in The Hooded Cloak in Macroom, when the band discovers that the crowd of ravers they are expecting turns out to be a group of Senior Citizens. Galaxy's drummer Jim Dwyer, who started his career banging two pokers off a cushion, shakes his head thinking about how their set went down like a lead balloon. 'Again, we broke into waltzes and did 'Rocking All Over the World' in waltz time, and they loved it! They came up demanding more, so we played more rubbish in three/four time. The one thing that saved the band: no matter how good or bad the gig was, we still gave it the full whack.'

Brian had been on the social committee of Bandon Rugby Club back in February 1983, and things weren't too exciting in the club socially at the time. He decided to inject some life into the scene by getting a band to play on Valentine's Night and rounded up a few musicians for the job, including Anthony O'Donovan on bass guitar, Jerry McSweeney on guitar, Jim Dwyer on guitar and Johnny Crowley on keyboard. Brian was the front man and vocalist. They rehearsed in the keg room at the back of Flor Crowley's bar.

Valentine's Night in the rugby club was planned as a pyjama party but everyone showed up in jeans and jerseys except Brian, who sat in his chair in his best striped flannels. The musicians went their separate ways after the gig but a few weeks later another musician, Gerry Lane, fell in with them for a performance at Flor Crowley's. This was the genesis of Galaxy. The band went through almost thirty musicians in its time but the four constants were Brian, Gerry Lane, Jim Dwyer and Noel Curran.

Jim Dwyer was working at Carberry Milk Products in Ballineen when Galaxy first got together. He sometimes worked the 2 pm to 10 pm shift, which was a problem. 'When we had a gig in Bandon at nine o'clock,' he relates, 'Brian would roar up in his car at about half eight. I'd do a runner out the window and across the front lawn of the factory, every supervisor in the place looking at me. I'd dive into Brian's car and we'd race off into Bandon – like a real secret agent style of operation. He was a murderous driver, being honest.'

Noel Curran was from Farranfree in Cork's working-class northside. A session guitar player, he had been playing with different showbands from his early teens. He was introduced to the band by Gerry Lane, with whom he had played in another outfit previously. Gerry was from Russell Hill in Upton, a small West Cork village best-known for its steam rally, its tulips and its facilities for the handicapped. He had caught the bug for playing music professionally back in 1974 when Noel Redding, Jimi Hendrix's bass guitarist, brought his car into the garage where Gerry was working. Gerry started with a showband called Discovery, later getting together a rock band called Driveshaft which played support to major acts like Rory Gallagher, Phil Lynott and Def Leppard. He was based in England and working with musicians such as Gary Moore and Queen's Brian May when Brian Crowley first told him he was starting a band and invited him to play with them. He came home every couple of months and played with the band, and when he returned to Bandon to live in 1987 he joined them full time.

The band got a boost in its early days when a new nightclub opened up in a hotel in Bandon, and the bus-loads of youngsters who came into town for the disco gathered in Flor Crowley's first to hear Galaxy. After cutting their milk teeth in Crowley's, Galaxy moved on to Shanley's in Clonakilty. It was a step forward. If Bandon is the stolid older sister with her feet firmly rooted in commerce and old money, Clonakilty is the jaunty young one with the sea breeze in her hair. Clonakilty has a sense of life about it, 'a happening town' in the same way that Galway is, and Shanley's Pub was at the heart of the local music scene. All the young people went there: locals, hippies, people on holidays. Brian of course was back in his father's old haunt, except that instead of holding a clinic in the back room, he was out front trying to raise the rafters.

With a little encouragement from Moss Shanley, Brian had sung in public for the first time in the summer of 1982. When he went back there with the band, Moss Shanley, a musician himself, often joined in the gig. A few years later, Moss and Brian would bring the house down with their version of 'Just a Gigolo'. Their approach to music was similar.

'You have fabulous musicians buried in a corner because they play highly technical stuff which will really only be appreciated by other musicians,' Moss says. 'Brian and myself always felt that if something became number one, a lot of people liked it, whether we did or not. It didn't matter what age a song was as long as it was number one, two or three in the charts at some stage. Brian is very hearty, very robust as a performer. As a vocalist, he'd be parallel to my delivery as a pianist, because I wouldn't be technically at the races, but bejasus you'd have no trouble hearing me.'

Once Galaxy began to play in Shanleys, it opened up to new influences. Gerry Lane knew the local network, and one night when he couldn't make a gig he promised the others, 'I'll get a guitar player for you.' Ten minutes before they were due to start, ex-Thin Lizzy guitarist Eric Bell walked in the door. Noel Redding, who had inspired Gerry originally, and who now lived in a big old house outside of Clonakilty, shaped the band a bit more. Clonakilty was like a nursery for Galaxy. They played there every Friday, Saturday and Sunday night, and when the pub closed they moved on to play in local dance halls and hotels. 'We were playing so much we started to get good,' Jim Dwyer says.

The money wasn't bad either. Brian was the manager and he understood how to make a deal. 'He said the more you charge, the more people respect you, and in music that's very true. You don't get any favours if you under-price yourself.' He set a price and that was it. He had no hesitation in asking for money. When they started out, they were getting £100 for Flor Crowley's and £150 for the rugby club.

'They were the cheapest things we ever did,' Brian says. 'I had a policy that each member of the band would get £40 an hour for playing. That was £80 for a gig. Then you had to add on the cost of petrol and roadies. We never did Cork for less than £600.'

While the others had been playing music since they were fourteen or fifteen, Brian was new to the business and he had some catching up to do. There were simple things such as keeping time with a song. Every musician 'keeps a leg going' when they are playing to help them keep the beat, but Brian couldn't do that and his timing wasn't great until Jim Dwyer taught him how to tap his left hand when he was singing. There were other things to catch up on as well.

'Brian learned very quickly,' Jim Dwyer said. 'If he makes a mistake once, he won't make it the second time. I was asked one night who my favourite singer was and I said Paul Rogers from Free. They asked Brian and he came up with somebody ridiculous like somebody out of the Dooleys. Everyone just laughed. A couple of months later the same conversation came up with a different group, and Brian was asked who his favourite singer was, and straight away he said it was Paul Rogers from Free. A cool customer – he immediately got approval for that. That's the way Brian operated, very, very quick in picking things up.'

If Brian was the mover when it came to money, the dominant influence musically was Gerry Lane, who had been playing professionally for years. In rehearsals he tightened up the songs and arranged the numbers. Under his guidance the band began to gel, playing technically difficult numbers from AC/DC, Whitesnake and Rainbow. They rehearsed their sets, but if somebody turned up with a new song, it was often a case of 'watch my leg for the stop' or 'watch my hand for the start'. When they started out, they were into the glam rock bands of the '80s. Then Gerry went into the blues, and so they all went into the blues.

With Jim Dwyer on drums, Noel Curran on bass and Gerry Lane on guitar, Brian fronted the show. As he grew in confidence, he developed his own style.

'Brian came from the political background where you have to be nice to people, you have to talk to people,' Jim Dwyer says. 'He brought that into the band and it worked very well. People were charmed and came up talking to him. He was a novelty as well, a guy in a wheelchair singing, but he had an ability to make people forget the wheelchair. After a while they just saw Brian. He got better then. He copied Gerry a lot for the getting-the-crowd-going techniques. I think he was second to none. He could keep a show going. If something went wrong, Brian would keep the talk going until we were ready to go again.'

While the band was growing in popularity, the Crowley household was patiently waiting for Brian to come back to reality, to get the music out of his system and find a reliable job. Niall, who had envisaged Brian as a solicitor or an accountant, could not identify with the music scene and often wondered what his long-haired brother was at. 'Anyone I saw who was associated with it – even fellows older than him – still hadn't their life on the road,' he says. 'Maybe they were happy in themselves, but I had different criteria. They looked like people who were directionless, living from day to day, week to week. I had no interest in music whatsoever. It was probably very good for Brian but I thought he was wasting his time.' Flor Junior had less philosophical grounds for finding fault with Galaxy. 'I put a disc out in my back lifting a trailer for his shagging band,' he will tell you.

For their part, Brian's musician friends thought the Crowleys a lovely family, very friendly and never slow to supply a meal or a bed for the night. But in the Crowley philosophy, you went to school, you went to college and you got a job. Jim Dwyer describes the meeting of the music world with the world of the Crowley household as a case of 'mutual shock'.

'There was one musician who stood in with us for a while,' he recalls. 'He stayed with the Crowleys. There was no problem, he stayed in the house. He had long hair, a very thin face and huge lips, child-bearing lips. He looked like an idiot; he was an idiot to be honest. I often wondered what the Crowleys really thought of it all. To them, you had a career. In the music business, it's a totally different scene altogether.'

After they had built a solid following in West Cork Galaxy began to look for gigs in the city, and eventually began to play in popular venues like de Lacey's, the Grand Parade Hotel and Nancy Spain's. Outside of Cork, they played in Limerick, Waterford, Killarney and Tralee. They played on the street and at festivals, and once they played for the Rose of Tralee as well. She was none too happy with their performance. As she waved and smiled bravely at the crowds lining the street, there was a cold wind raising goose pimples on her bare shoulders and arms. As if to compound her misery, a group of jerks on the back of a lorry beside her float began trying to chat her up. When the parade ground to a halt, the guys wanted to know what she'd like to hear them play for her. Nope, they couldn't do any songs about San Francisco. Then, a blinding flash of inspiration and they blasted into Guns 'n Roses 'Welcome to the Jungle.' As the floats move on again, the San Fransisco Rose's ears start ringing.

One of the haunts of Cork musicians was a cafe run by Joe Mac of the Dixies showband in the Queen's Old Castle shopping centre. Across the river was Pa Johnson's Pub in Sawmills Street where 'all the heads' gathered on Monday nights when musicians from different bands took the floor in jamming sessions. Another discovery of Brian's was the 147 Snooker Club. When he held a snooker cue in his hand, Brian's competitive streak came out strongly; he played to win, every time. But because he was in a wheelchair he couldn't reach a certain spot in the middle of the table, and if you left the white ball sitting in the central area, he had to stretch for it using a cue-rest. His mates played on this weakness, constantly placing the white out of Brian's reach, but they admired the fact that he never cracked up about it.

On the road, Brian and Gerry played cards constantly, with the gear as the stake. One week Gerry owned all the gear, the next week it transferred to Brian. Mostly they played blackjack, and developed a kind of sign language – a collection of grunts and hand signals – that signalled when they were raising the stakes or staying. The two of them had become close friends. Initially, Gerry thought Brian's positive outlook, his persistent optimism, was a bit of a show, an image he put on so that people wouldn't feel sorry for him. But he grew to realise that Brian's optimism was for real, and to admire the fact that though Brian had taken serious knocks in his life, he still held his head above the waterline.

Now almost full time on the road, Brian was becoming absorbed in the music world. It suited his instincts. He was earning good money and he had the freedom to do as he liked. He could stay in bed all day and stay out all night. He had always been a late-night person – in school he couldn't even attempt a maths question until after midnight. He enjoyed the *flaithiúlach* attitude to life and the sense of affinity between musicians. One of the big nights on his calendar was the

Monday of Cork's jazz week, when the festival was over and the bands who were in town gathered for a final session in the Grand Parade Hotel.

Though he was quite naive when he started out, he was around long enough to grow aware of the downside of the free-wheeling life: the lack of secure relationships or steady income, the delusions and the defeats. Drink was the major drug. Soft drugs were popular, sometimes more so with the people who hung around the bands trying to be cool than with the musicians themselves. Brian was offered hash once or twice; after that word got round that he didn't use it. He saw some victims of hard-drug dependency, one man who was addicted to heroin 'dying in front of my eyes', though he later got treatment and put his life back together.

Whatever about the difficulties of making it or the reservations of his family, always at the back of his mind was the idea that they were going to make it big. Even though he realised his own limitations as a performer and Galaxy's limitations as a group, that dream was always there.

'It never leaves,' he says. 'That's the one thing that keeps you going all the time, the fact that you could be the next Beatles, the next U2 or whatever.'

Whatever about the future's promise, Brian's friend John Hurley felt that the band fulfilled one very important function in the present. 'When he was singing out his heart and soul, I think he forgot everything else. It was his escape.'

Brian disagrees with that interpretation. 'I wanted to get into the band, to do it, to experience the applause and the control; that's a big thing, the ego-boosting is enormous. Likewise, the ego deflation is enormous when the gig doesn't work. The highs and lows are phenomenal. Even playing in a pub, if you get a good reaction, there's such a brilliant buzz from that, it takes you hours to come down.'

As the band made a name for itself as a punchy rock/blues

band, Brian developed a new identity as a singer. He became known for himself in a milieu where Fianna Fáil politics were as foreign as Egyptian hieroglyphics.

'I wasn't a good guitar player, a good drummer or a good piano player,' he says. 'I couldn't do that. I was a good singer, not brilliant, but I was a brilliant front person. That's where my talent was, as a good front man. The band gave me a self-identity and a name in my own right more than anything else.' But only in some circles. He was still Flor Crowley's son in others.

There was a lot of energy in the band. They thumped it out at the loudest volume possible, setting ears ringing for days afterwards. The gear was wrecked. They were playing regularly, doing well if not getting famous. They didn't take themselves too seriously, and the *craic* was always good. Brian's voice was strong and getting better. He did a particularly good version of 'Mustang Sally', a song made popular by the film, *The Commitments*. But he didn't always get the songs spot on. Five minutes before a gig on New Year's Eve in Nancy Spain's in Cork, the band was rehearsing Auld Lang Syne. Noel knew something was wrong with the key – it was too high for Brian. 'If you heard him, it was unbelievable,' he recalls. 'The minute he finished there was dead silence. It must have been one of the worst ever entries to a New Year. We got the tape back of the gig and I thought it was the funniest thing I ever heard. I gave Brian a loan of it but when I came to that part afterwards, it was gone.'

At open-air gigs like the Rose of Tralee, the rest of the band would lift Brian on to the truck; at basement or first floor venues they carted him up and down the stairs. Four guys playing together, travelling together, slagging one another mercilessly, comforting each others' egos. They had their fights in the band, too, needling one another, drawing one another out. Brian had a temper, but more often he took a diplomatic approach to incidents. 'At a gig, we might start arguing about a song. Brian would say, "Let's argue about this afterwards".' As manager Brian made sure things ran on time, that the gig was advertised, that there was money for petrol. It was a handy way out for the other band members when they wanted to unload bores or drunks: talk to him, he's the boss. But at times his forbearance seemed too much.

Jim Dwyer is standing beside the wheelchair while Brian is talking to a girl in a dance hall at the end of a night. Jim catches a phrase of the conversation. It sounds like 'you can't do that anyway' or 'you can't get it up'. Then she walks away. Jim wants to go over and kill her, but Brian just says, 'Leave her off.'

Another night in Crookstown after a Macra 'do', an old bore comes over to Brian and asks repeatedly, 'What happened to you? You're in a chair!' Jim tells him what to do with himself, but Brian makes no response. A woman drags the old man away eventually.

'He's very even-tempered, always outgoing, always pleasant,' Jim relates. 'I don't think I ever saw him losing it. Occasionally, he would just go quiet and into himself.'

The band head to Dingle for a weekend during the 1990 World Cup. The lads are on the piss, in and out of pubs all day. Brian is dragged along in their wake, though he's not drinking. At about six o'clock in the evening, 'he gets a sudden attack of religion'. He just wants to go to the church, and asks Jim if he'll push him up the hill.

'There was this bloody hill, it was *that* steep. I nearly got a heart attack. I didn't want to be pushing him up the hill. What I do remember particularly, though, was that he had a long day and he wanted some time away on his own. He could just get like that at times, quiet.'

NOEL Curran used to wonder why Brian couldn't turn up for a game of snooker until half six on a Sunday evening. When he asked him about it, Brian explained that he went to mass first. That's how Noel found out that Brian's religious faith was an important part of his life; other than that, Brian never made an issue of it. For Noel, his friend's religious commitment was something to be admired.

Brian hadn't lost his spiritual side. If anything, prayer had become more a part of the fabric of his day-to-day life since his accident. He found it an enriching experience, something he got a return from. The big return was the inner belief and confidence that no matter what may happen it would work out all right, and if it didn't he would still be able to deal with it. Prayer wasn't limited to formal situations for him. There would be nothing to stop him from just having a chat with God when he was driving back from somewhere on his own. He preferred to be on his own when he prayed, rather than with a congregation. He went to mass and got something from that, but he really enjoyed praying on his own. It seemed more personal.

Brian had found a soul-mate in Grattan Neville, a Clonakilty man who had a reputation for enjoying the *craic* and yet, beneath the surface, shared an openness to life's spiritual dimension. Grattan, a solicitor in his forties, knew Brian from the rugby circuit in West Cork. One Wednesday night he rang Brian up out of the blue and asked him if he wanted to go away for the weekend. Grattan had a name for being a wild man and his weekend tears were legendary, so Brian was chuffed to be invited along and said he'd love to go. Then Grattan asked him if he prayed and had he ever been to Medjugorje. By the weekend, they were flying into Sarajevo. En route through Heathrow, Brian's wheelchair was taken apart by airport security staff for the very first time. He felt that the search, and subsequent searches, were linked to his republican sympathies, though of course he could never know for sure.

Yugoslavia was a popular holiday destination when Brian touched down there in 1985 with Grattan and his daughter,

Jackie, but they were going there as pilgrims rather than holiday-makers. Grattan was looking for something in his life at the time and had an instinctive feeling that he might find it in Medjugorje.

They stayed overnight in Mostar, hired a car and drove next day to the village where, four years earlier, six local children had announced that Our Lady had appeared to them. A drive of about two and a half hours brought them through spectacularly beautiful scenery in the mountains of the former Yugoslavia, now know as the Republic of Bosnia-Hercegovina. Medjugorje's popularity as a place of pilgrimage was evident in the number of buses on route to the isolated mountain village, and the spiritual experience touching the lives of those living in the area was to be seen on the hands of the local people, who carried rosary beads as they worked in the tobacco fields and herded their sheep. As they reached the village, they saw priests sitting out in the fields hearing confessions, while long lines of people queued before them.

Brian was sceptical. He had faith, belief, but he was uncomfortable with the idea of 'visions'.

When they arrived in Medjugorje, Brian and the Nevilles met a nun from the local convent, Sr Yianni, whom Brian knew through a contact in Dublin. Sr Yianni, who had learned English from an Irish Franciscan and spoke with a Galway accent, arranged for them to be among a group of about thirty people present with the five visionaries in the sacristy of the basilica. The room had plain white walls and a wooden floor. The visionaries knelt in front of a marble altar with a statue of Our Lady on it. Brian was one of three people facing the visionaries.

'Half way through their praying they dropped to their knees and went into a trance of some kind. It went on for about twenty minutes and then they came out of the visions separately. Each of them acted differently. One or two of them had their eyes open and they were speaking; one said nothing. They were all looking at the same point. When they came out of the visions, they went back saying the rosary. I knew there was certainly something there; what it was I don't know. You could feel a presence. It was like no emotion I had known before or since. It was something totally unique or different.

'What amazed me most of all was that the visionaries were such ordinary people. I met one of the girls, Maria, when we arrived. She was in wellington boots, cleaning out a hay barn with a pitchfork. An hour later she was having a vision. The simplicity and the power of the place was enormous.' He left Medjugorje with a sense of peace and well-being that he found difficult to define.

Grattan, for his part, went back there several times. People said he had flipped, because he spoke so much about Medjugorje and began to show videos of the place to his friends, but after a while people who knew him realised it meant something remarkable to him. He was still the same Grattan, full of life and fun, but 'he just got an inner grace, an inner happiness that was so visible'.

That inner peace and strength remained with Grattan Neville in the following years when he learned that his life would be cut short by cancer. Two days before he died, he stopped at Craigie on his way home from hospital. He wasn't able to get out of the car and Brian went out to talk to him. Brian believes that Grattan drew strength from his faith and his belief. 'Even when he knew he was dying, he felt he was ready to go and he had no fear.'

Grattan was in his fifties and had been appointed a district justice by the time he died in 1990. Despite the gap in their ages, he and Brian had grown to be close friends. His death left a sense of loss and sorrow which were tempered by 'the knowledge that he was going to a better place'.

Whatever others may have thought of his beliefs, Brian was happy to go his own way on it. From childhood he had been

known as Flor Crowley's son. After the accident he was the
Crowley boy that fell off the roof and was in a wheelchair. His
first jobs – in the bar and the auctioneering office – were part of
the family business. He ploughed his own furrow with the band,
and if he wasn't afraid to take a different course from what his
family would have liked, neither was he going to worry about
being different in this new milieu.

Chapter Six

URING THE TIME Brian was immersed in the music world, he still kept up his involvement in politics. For the other members of the band, music dominated everything else, but Brian had a political mind. 'We might have a foot in reality every now and again,' Jim Dwyer says, 'but Brian always knew. He was always working towards something else.'

Brian would often find himself explaining the vagaries of proportional representation or justifying the machinations of the party system to his friends in the band. They would sometimes argue about the issues of the day, and if their discussions occasionally became heated, they were doing no more than echoing the voices raised in public debate all around them. Throughout the 1980s, as modernisation brought with it a new social code, conservatives and liberals battled over issues of public morality and the kind of society Ireland would have in the future. In 1983 the Fine Gael–Labour coalition introduced an amendment to the constitution with the aim of making the existing ban on abortion irrevocable; the pro-life amendment, as it was called, was carried after a very angry and divisive campaign. Three years later, when a referendum to remove the constitution's ban on divorce was held, this liberal attempt was lost at the polls.

While the issues and the main players could be, and often were, typecast to fit the usual categories – young or old, urban or rural, progressive or traditional – the ongoing national debate involved questions of public and personal values which touched everyone individually. Brian was in favour of the pro-life amendment and he opposed divorce. He did not believe, either, that the wording of the amendment was flawed, as was later argued when the Supreme Court allowed for abortion to be carried out in certain circumstances. 'The amendment was all right, but the interpretation by the court was wrong,' he insists. 'The Dáil should have brought in legislation so that there could be no dispute over the interpretation. I believe abortion is wrong.' A number of years later he canvassed for and voted in favour of the 1993 referendum, an alteration to the earlier provisions, which allowed women the freedom to travel abroad for abortions and to have access to information on abortion services.

Brian may have been travelling the roads with a rock band, but he had not altogether strayed outside the fold, and he continued to go to Fianna Fáil meetings and visit the Dáil. The party had assumed an aspect of calm, on the surface at least, after Haughey, the great survivor, had defied the pundits and routed the challengers to his leadership in 1983. Back in government from 1987 to 1989, Fianna Fáil implemented stringent economic policies which earned the Crowleys' old house-guest, Ray MacSharry, then Minister for Finance, the nickname 'Mac the Knife'. Haughey's personality dominated Irish politics, galvanising the opposition into tirades of anti-Haughey feeling, but a watershed in the history of the party was reached in 1989 when it joined forces with the Progressive Democrats in its first ever coalition, marking the decline of Fianna Fáil as the country's great political monolith.

Brian was not involved in the Fianna Fáil organisation in West Cork – he was loath to support the TD who had taken his father's seat – but he was a member of the Knockavilla Cumann based just outside Bandon. He was a committed Fianna Fáil activist, attending the Árd Fheis, canvassing for members seeking election to the national executive, campaigning for the party at elections. He worked for the party's Dáil candidates in the city constituency and supported Gene Fitzgerald in the European elections in 1989. He canvassed for Brian Lenihan in Cork, Kerry, Waterford and Tipperary during the presidential election campaign of 1990 which ended in a debacle for the Fianna Fáil candidate.

But for all his preoccupation with politics and his hectic life with the band, Brian's life wasn't full until a friendship which first began during the sessions in Shanley's grew to become something infinitely deeper and more personal.

Una O'Sullivan was a friend of Yvonne Shanley's, one of the gang who came to the bar to hear Galaxy at weekends. She was eighteen and taking a secretarial course. A tall, brown-haired girl with a quiet manner, she was a good singer and interested in music. They were drawn to each other's company and found themselves spending hours talking together in the bar. When they first started going out, Brian was playing it cool. He was twenty-three and not too keen on a serious relationship.

A year after they began seeing one another, they split up when Una went to work in Germany for the summer. In the three months she was away, Brian did some soul-searching. He wrote a song, 'She's My Woman', which the band recorded in Noel Redding's studio in his house outside Clonakilty; later they submitted it for the National Song Contest. It was about her going away and Brian's discovering the depths of his feeling for her by his sense of loss in her absence. When she returned home, Una found to her astonishment that he was really attracted to her. Soon they were meeting every day, or talking on the phone to one another constantly. 'We had a lot in common, and I could tell him anything,' Una recalls. 'He was totally my best friend.'

Brian had long developed the habit of dealing with his feelings internally, of keeping his thoughts to himself; he may have been the one friends felt they could pour their troubles out to, but on personal matters he preferred to keep his own counsel. 'You'll never get anything out of Brian that he doesn't want to give you,' John Hurley says of him. But as his relationship with Una evolved, he found himself exploring new ground where he had to leave himself exposed.

At the start of any new relationship there is always apprehension as to how much of yourself you have to give, compounded by a fear of being hurt or rejected in the future. When Brian began to grow more involved with Una, he found that 'there has to be confidence, and a confiding of thoughts, and I had a fear of having to do that'.

When Una moved to Cork to train as a hairdresser, they continued to meet often. Una would travel with Brian to gigs, and banned smoking in the car, despite all protests. On the way to a gig in West Cork, Una begins to sing 'Summertime' and Brian takes the song up, singing in seconds as they drive. 'New York, New York' and Jimmy McCarthy's 'Ride On' are special favourites, and at a gig one night Una gets up on stage and they duet on 'I Can See Clearly Now'. At the end of the night in Shanley's, Brian would go off to Una's, Jim O'Dwyer in tow. At two in the morning, Jim would still be sitting in Brian's car, waiting for him to come out of the house so that they could go home. He'd go and bang on the door and Brian would call, 'I'll be out in a minute!' Three o'clock and they'd still be there. 'They were very, very close,' Jim says.

Sometimes they would drive late at night to a favourite cove, listening to the sound of the waves hitting the rocks below and music low on the car stereo. Talking and looking out at the stars, they spent hours there, often not leaving until the early morning. 'I used to love that,' Una remembers. 'It was a lovely time.' They went to concerts and the cinema, out for meals or occasionally to see a play, and they went on holidays to Portugal. Una worked on her tan while Brian hid in the shade.

For their first Valentine's Day together, Brian sent Una twelve red roses. The number multiplied to twenty-four, thirty-six and forty-eight in the following years. 'He totally spoiled me – completely. It was far too much really, sometimes. Because he wasn't working, he was at my beck and call, which used to drive me crazy as well, because I'd have loved if he did more for himself then.' Yet she admired Brian's giving attitude and his positive outlook on life. She remembers him in the city on a cold, wintry night. They were stopped at traffic lights when they noticed a down-and-out sheltering in a bus-stop, and spontaneously Brian rolled down the car window and handed him some money out of his pocket. In their four years together, Una could count on one hand the number of times Brian got fed up about things. Before she came to know him well, she felt he couldn't be so good-humoured all the time, but: 'Four years is a long time seeing each other so often. You'd have to catch him on a bad day, and they were very few and far between.' Kidney infections, which still hit him from time to time, got him down, but otherwise he was simply a very happy, upbeat guy.

As Una got to know Brian, she saw more and more how privately he guarded his thoughts and feelings. Brian opened up when he spoke to her and to Gerry Lane, but she didn't feel he had the same level of intimacy with anyone else. 'It does take him a while to allow people to come in. But if you're in, then you're a friend for ever more.'

As a deeper confidence developed between them, Brian found there was nothing he couldn't tell her. He couldn't lie to her, couldn't hide if she asked him a question. One of Brian's anxieties was about the wheelchair. At the start it hadn't made a difference, but he felt it began to create difficulties as the relationship progressed. There were things Una wanted to do that he couldn't, simple things, like going horse-riding for an afternoon. There were things they couldn't share because of his disability. But it wasn't actually of such great concern to Una; she like him for the person he was, and valued the strength of their friendship. He was good to have as a friend. If she were down, or feeling she hadn't the ability to accomplish something she wanted, he would encourage her until eventually she would overcome her reluctance and discover her own energy and confidence.

Three years into the relationship, Una went to Dublin a week after her twenty-first birthday to do a course, and when she was offered a job in the city she decided to take it. At first she was terribly homesick and really hated Dublin, but when she made new friends that began to change. There was a subtle change in their relationship as well. Una began to feel that she needed more space for herself. Looking back on that time, she feels she was 'terribly immature' when she knew Brian, who was her very first boyfriend. Her friends said she should see more of life.

For the time being Una suppressed her misgivings and continued seeing Brian regularly. When he didn't come to Dublin, she travelled home. But they had begun to disagree about things, especially the band and Brian's lifestyle. Una would give out to him about the band, his lack of direction, the fact that he should be doing something else besides singing. Like a lot of people she felt the band wasn't a real job, whereas in Brian's mind it was, because he was working hard and making good money at it.

Una began to take the long view, to think ahead. She began to think seriously about the implications if they were to plan a future together. She always wanted to have children but she didn't know if Brian and herself would be able to have a child naturally. She asked Brian a few times to find out when he went into hospital for check-ups. 'I'd say, "When you're in, just see," and he never did. Whether he did and it wasn't very positive and he didn't tell me, I don't know. He just never got back to me.'

But Brian had given a lot of thought to the possibility of his and Una's having children if they decided to marry. 'I thought it could be overcome and it wasn't an inhibiting factor. I personally feel that physical difficulties are easier to overcome than the mental difficulties people have in a relationship. I would love to have children. Of course there would be a physical difficulty in creating children, but it's not insurmountable, and there's a proven track record now of treatment that can assist in that. I wouldn't see that as an inhibiting factor for my future in that sense. The biggest problem for me is to find the right person.'

In February 1990, they went to see Eric Clapton in concert in London. Brian had sold a raffle ticket to a friend of Una's who, having won a few thousand pounds in the draw, paid for the London trip as a gift in return. After they arrived back in Dublin, Brian went to Leinster House to listen to Finance Minister Albert Reynolds introduce the budget, and then he called into Una's to say goodbye before heading for home. He was late leaving and the weather was dreadful, so windy that the car was shaking. He stopped in Cashel to rest for an hour and then got back on the road. Just outside Cork he turned down the hill on to a straight stretch of road at Watergrasshill. The wind was gusting to 110 mph.

Suddenly he had no control of the car. It seemed as if it had just been picked up and flung across the road. It rolled down an embankment, turning over twice before landing at the bottom on all four wheels.

Brian's first thought was, 'I hope to God I'm not after breaking my neck.' He discovered he could move one of his hands. All his injuries seemed to be concentrated on his right side. He had a lot of of difficulty breathing because his ribs were broken. His right arm was very painful.

He turned the ignition but the car wouldn't start. He dialled for help on the car-phone, but that wasn't working either. He heard lorries passing on the main road and blew the horn, but failed to alert any passing traffic. The dawn was slow in coming. He grew cold in the pitch dark and took another jacket out of the suitcase behind him to try to keep warm. He began to control his breathing, breathing in, counting for ten seconds, exhaling. He didn't have any thoughts of death or dying, but he was growing weaker and beginning to feel terribly cold.

Bill Saich, who worked with the Automobile Association in Cork, was driving in from Mitchelstown to work when he noticed a disturbance in the low ditch beside the road. He pulled in and saw the car below. He shouted down. Brian took a red handkerchief from the top pocket of his suit jacket and waved it through the broken sun roof. Bill Saich flagged down a lorry driver to stay with Brian while he went to contact the emergency services.

The fire brigade and ambulance arrived and began cutting through the door of the car. Shards of glass from the shattered sun roof had cut Brian's face; blood was soaking through his shirt. The door was pulled away, and as the men moved in to carefully prise him out from behind the steering wheel, Brian told them that he was paralysed.

'Don't worry, you'll be grand,' one of the men reassured him.

'But I *am* paralysed,' Brian insisted.

'You'll be OK. We'll have you in hospital in no time.'

'Look!' He pointed to the wheelchair in the back of the car.

Bill Saich's intervention had made the difference between life and death. If Brian had been found half an hour later, he would have been in a coma as a result of hypothermia. Even when he was brought into hospital, it was touch and go. For two and a half days his family waited anxiously, angry too that this should have happened again.

He was able to tell the doctors which injuries were old ones, which gave them extra time to do other work they had to do. His collar bone had come out through his skin. He had broken five ribs on the right hand side and each one was broken in three places. He had five punctures in the lung. The real threat was from lung collapse and hypothermia. He was put on a ventilator; drains were attached to his lungs and chest. He was getting blood transfusions and there was a drip for antibiotics and fluids. The doctors estimated he would be on a life support machine for at least a month, in hospital for three months.

While he was on the life support machine and on lung drains, he was kept sedated to prevent his dislodging the tubes, but because he began fighting against the treatment he was negating the effects of the morphine. They gave him more of it to keep him sedated, but that created another problem: when they reduced the high dosages, he began to suffer withdrawal symptoms. In a hallucinatory state, he thought he was in hospitals in Dublin and London and became frightened.

He began to think that the doctors were going to kill him. They would tell his parents, 'Well, sorry about this. He died from his injuries.' He had never been more scared in his life. The paranoia may have stemmed from his overhearing that some patients had died in the Intensive Care Unit while he was there.

He attempted to discharge himself. He summoned a doctor and told him he couldn't deny him the right to discharge himself. 'I want my lawyer in now and I want a taxi,' he thundered. He couldn't sleep for fear he would be killed while he slept. He lay in bed watching the ads on the television, though there was no TV in the room. At one stage, he got it into his mind that one of the doctors was going to inject him with meningitis but that the injection would only be fatal if the doctor touched him afterwards. When the doctor came around, he pulled out the drips attached to his body and tried to escape from the bed. He couldn't move. He caught an aerosol of aftershave and began spraying the doctors to keep them at bay. They quietened him down and replaced the drips. A doctor gave him an injection. 'Tell me why are you doing this to me,' he asked them. 'Is it religious, or for money or what?'

Seven days after the accident, it was felt he had made enough progress to be taken off the life support machine. A day or so later, with great difficulty and great pain, he was able to get out of bed and into the wheelchair. He was in desperate agony just pushing around the place, but he was self-assured, even cocky, about the accident and his ability to deal with it. 'The reason it probably happened to me was that He knew I could handle it. If it had happened somebody else, it might have killed them.'

He just wanted to go home, and about ten days after he had totalled the car, he left hospital. Mrs O'Callaghan greeted him in typically acerbic manner: 'That's what you get now for your dirty weekend in London.'

He went through three weeks of physiotherapy at home. He was socialising and driving by Easter, but it was the beginning of May before he was fully back in action, and he had missed a lot of time with the band because his vocal chords had been damaged by one of the tubes in his throat.

When Una had sat beside Brian's bedside in the hospital in Cork and listened to his shallow breathing as he lay there unconscious, she had made a promise that she would marry him. The trauma of Brian's near death forged a new closeness between them and the tensions which had been emerging in their relationship were pushed into the background – temporarily. 'Maybe if I was different and she was different, we would have thought about marriage, but I think that my own subconscious would have stopped me at that time. Before my accident, there wasn't much going on between us. The accident put that pressure on hold, but it would have resurfaced again. In that sense, we both realised we were coming near the end.'

During the summer they began to drift apart. While Una knew things weren't right between them, she hadn't specifically been thinking of breaking up. When Brian came up to Dublin one weekend, she told him she needed a break. 'I was probably a little bit suffocated. I just wanted to do some things on my own as well. Because it was every weekend and sometimes during the week, probably for the first time I felt a little bit suffocated and I just wanted to be on my own for a while.' She wondered if she were doing the right thing, sometimes thinking, 'Well, I'm not going to meet as nice a guy ever again,' but she had moved too far away from him by now. In the end the break became final when Una met somebody else.

Breaking up was difficult and they both felt hurt, at a loss, and missed the security of their long companionship. It took Brian longer to get over missing Una than he admitted to himself. The biggest hurt really was the loss of someone with whom he had built confidence and trust. 'Not only was I involved in a relationship with her but she was also my best friend. That's what hurt most when the relationship broke up – it was the loss of a friend.'

Una knew she had hurt Brian badly and she was sorry that she was the one who had done that, but the break-up had been painful for her as well. She made him promise that, by September of the following year, he would get a 'proper job' and not go on wasting his time with the band. 'He does keep a promise, that's one thing about him.'

Brian told her, 'Of course, if you need help or someone to talk to, I'll be there,' even though, in saying it, he knew that it was over between them. They did keep in contact with one another.

'He was always there for me. If ever there was anything wrong, I'd ring Brian for a long, long time afterwards. For a long time, and it was a bit unfair really...'

Gerry Lane knew the story. He had gone through a similar patch in his own life. The side of Brian most people saw was the happy-go-lucky, jolly side, but he and Gerry shared their deeper feelings. If Brian felt any self-doubt or worried that someone without a disability could have offered Una a fuller life, he managed to come to terms with it. He did not regard it as a factor, 'because I don't think there is any such thing as perfection. There would be similar difficulties in other relationships I had or I may have. If you find someone you love and you like, those difficulties can be overcome.'

Brian knew that he had shared something very special with
Una. He didn't want doubt to mar that feeling. Neither did he
feel cynical about the possibility of future relationships; if anything it made him more positive, showed him 'that this was
attainable, that you could reach this level of togetherness with
somebody.

'I'm not of the opinion there's only one person in the world
for you and you either find that person or you don't. I think
there are several people you find, and who will change your life
in some way.'

There was a difference in Brian after the break-up with Una.
He was quieter in himself. 'After Una he started to change a bit,'
Jim Dwyer relates. 'I suppose he started to grow up. You see,
music can be very fake as well. You need to have other interests,
other outlets.'

By now the band was starting to go down, too. There were
fewer venues and other younger bands coming up. Brian was
becoming dissatisfied with it; music can be a hard grind, playing
in grubby pubs, listening to drunks. Brian wanted more out of
life. It was tough getting work by this stage. In 1988, Galaxy
had a choice of 198 venues around the country, but two years
later this had fallen to just twenty-six. Brian could see the writing on the wall. He toyed with the idea of changing the style of
the band for a while, but then he saw an advertisement in a
newspaper.

'I just saw this ad,' he says. 'Again, whether it is the Higher
Power at work or whatever, I saw it at the right time and I got it.
It opened up a whole new range of opportunities beyond my
wildest expectations.'

Chapter Seven

L AW WOULD HAVE been his first choice if he had gone to college after he left school. Now he rediscovered his interest through a newspaper advertisement inviting mature students to apply for a degree course in University College Cork. Brian was no stranger to the place – he had often called into the university when Niall was a student there – and the course appealed to the night owl in him; lectures were held on Monday, Tuesday, Wednesday and Thursday evenings, which left days and weekends free. In the autumn of 1991, just over a year after Una had extracted a promise from him to find a 'proper job', he took his place in the lecture hall. He wasn't sure how he was going to get on, but he was going to give it a try at least.

The band had been on a downward spiral for a year or more. Karaoke, the killer singers, had taken over in many pub venues and it was hard to get work that paid well. Jim and Noel had begun to gig with other bands and Gerry, who had returned to Ireland after many years living across the water, was thinking about emigrating again. Brian continued to sing with bands when he started in college, and he did a few gigs in Shanley's with Gerry before he headed off to Spain. He also did some property valuations for solicitors in Bandon. As well, he had the compensation he had received after his first accident, so that, even with the band on the wane and hefty college fees to pay, he

99

didn't go through lean times during his student days. In any case, living at home, his expenses were low.

Barry Manley was working in Spain when Brian wrote to him and told him about the law course. Like most of his friends, Barry was delighted with the development. 'He was interested in law. He enjoyed music, but he needed more than that. Law didn't interfere with his music anyway. Politics was the only thing that interfered terminally with that.' Barry felt that the second accident had been a big influence on Brian. 'He had another close brush with death. He saw then that all this tearing around at five in the morning would have to stop.'

When Brian arrived in UCC he looked the part, with long hair and a battered leather jacket that had seen better days. He had to be lifted into some of the lecture halls in his wheelchair and sat in the front of the auditoriums because it was the most convenient place. It helped to keep his attention focused. He felt as if he were starting school again, but the atmosphere of the lecture theatre and the library, the smell of new books, crisp white pages unfolding ideas and complex principles of law, soon drew him in. His nocturnal nature suited his transition from singer to student. When he returned home to Bandon after lectures, he would stay up until the small hours writing up his notes.

He began to find different areas of law hugely relevant to aspects of his life. Because of his background in auctioneering, he took a particular interest in the law of conveyancing. Constitutional law was absorbing because of his political background, and when he daydreamed during lectures it was of becoming a barrister specialising in constitutional issues. The relevance of studying the law of tort, which deals with personal injuries and accidents, could not have been clearer. Between the covers of McMahon and Binchy's *A Case Book on the Law of Torts*, he discovered not an abstract legal case, but an account of his accident in *Crowley v. AIB*.

The legal action arising out of his accident had been heard before the High Court in 1985. Bandon solicitor Tony Neville, brother of Grattan Neville, was part of a strong Fianna Fáil legal team acting for the Crowleys. The late Niall McCarthy was chosen as Brian's senior counsel and, when he was appointed a judge of the High Court, was replaced by a former Fianna Fáil general election candidate, Aidan Browne. The second senior counsel was Colum Condon, who had been attorney general when Jack Lynch was Taoiseach, and the junior counsel was Dublin Fianna Fáil TD David Andrews. Brian sat at the hearings, alternately awed by the solemnity of the court and bored with its slow procedure. He enjoyed the pomp and ceremony, the tipstaff walking through the corridors calling out where the judge would be. He followed the hearings closely, noting the kinds of questions asked and points made, and he was impressed by the judge's clarity and humour.

The case before Judge Liam Hamilton was part-heard and settled out of court. Fault for the accident was apportioned between AIB and Brian Crowley as ninety-one per cent against the defendant and nine per cent against the plaintiff. The High Court judgment initially apportioned thirty per cent of the blame for the accident to the architects who designed the extension to the bank building, but they succeeded in dissociating themselves from the action on appeal. *Crowley v. AIB* subsequently became a case study in the law's reckoning of negligent liability.

Brian was awarded £125,000 for his injuries. He was twenty-one, but there was no mad spending spree. Bills had to be paid – work to the house and the cost of his car – and he used some of the money to help out at home financially. The balance was kept on deposit in a high-interest account. He invested some money in shares and bonds but says his investment in shares was not very prudent. There was no change in his lifestyle; he didn't start throwing his money around. He didn't change his car for four years after receiving the award.

Sitting at the front of the class literally put Brian to the fore, and in any case he was not slow to assert himself. He had a good rapport with his lecturers and became a class representative in his second year. His fellow students came from all backgrounds – there was a mix of guards, priests, businessmen, doctors and bank staff – and they were of all ages, the eldest in his 70s. Ninety people started the course; some took it to diploma level, finishing after two years, and some switched to other courses. About sixty-five completed the final year.

Strangers for the first few lectures, individuals within the class soon gathered in smaller groups, and Brian fell in with a circle which included Dermot Clancy, Siobhan Hanley and Gerard O'Mahony. They began to study together on Sunday evenings, building a framework of mutual support, which was important to mature students, none of whom had faced a school-type situation since they were in their teens. When he met the others for their Sunday study sessions, Brian must have felt a strong sense of déjà vu. Gerard O'Mahony had organised a room for them at Cork University Hospital, one of Brian's old alma maters.

Every Sunday evening in the quietness of that room, they pored over their lecture notes and discussed issues, developing relationships with one another in the process of studying law. In the study sessions and lectures, over cups of coffee and pints, wider questions of politics and culture came up for discussion and debate. In the exchange of ideas, the accommodation of viewpoints, and the contemplation of attitudes wildly different or strikingly similar to his own, Brian Crowley began to get into the stride of university life. He enjoyed the novelty, 'the whole newness of getting to know a different circle of people with different attitudes.'

Social get-togethers among the class were usually confined to Christmas or after exams, but occasionally Brian, Dermot Clancy and Ger O'Mahony went to a pub or restaurant together. Brian was a party man, always ready to pitch in with a

song. 'He is exceptionally good company,' Dermot Clancy says.
'He doesn't drink, but he's great fun. He was always up with
what was happening in UCC: politics, the bit of scandal or
whatever. His temper never varied. You'd never see Brian looking
stressed.' Dermot found Brian sociable, but did not think of
him as an extrovert. 'He was disabled. If you wanted to have a
conversation with him, you had to go towards Brian simply
because of his disability. I never really thought of him as an
extrovert, though he was always friendly and approachable. I'm
sure he has a private side in the sense that still waters run deep.'

Brian's disability was taken for granted by his fellow students,
who had never known him otherwise, but once in a while they
discovered the difficulty it could cause for him. Leaving Dermot's
house one night, Brian was negotiating the flight of steps outside
the door with some help from Dermot when a sudden jerk cata-
pulted him out of the wheelchair and he fell on the ground like a
rag doll. Dermot panicked, not knowing what to do.

'Brian stayed totally relaxed and directed me on how to get
him up. He was unflummoxed by the whole thing. You know
yourself, if you slip on the street, it doesn't improve your
humour, so I really admired Brian for his approach. He had
great sense of balance and equilibrium.'

As the year progressed, his new-found friends discovered
another quality in Brian. 'Brian is very, very competitive,'
Dermot Clancy says. 'One year, I got a mark slightly higher than
him and he wondered how in the name of God I beat him. I just
said it was easy enough and he laughed.'

Seeing a young man out at nights playing gigs, who had long
hair and who dressed like Brian did, Dermot expected that he
would naturally follow certain liberal perspectives – it came as a
shock to find that he had great devotion to Our Lady and was
opposed to divorce. If anything about his new friend came close
to annoying Dermot, this did.

'I was in favour of divorce; Brian was opposed to it. Brian was devoted to Our Lady; something that's totally alien to me. He has very traditional rural Ireland views. Ultimately, they are very Fianna Fáil views, and Brian is extremely convinced of them, without being dogmatic. A lot of the time we agreed to differ. He wasn't a craw-thumper. He expressed his opinions as he was entitled to and didn't get people's backs up. He didn't lecture about his views, he stayed above them. He wouldn't tell you about his religious conviction unless you asked him a question about it. He wasn't proselytising. Brian is ultimately the same person I first met, but his thinking comes from his traditional background. There is nothing wrong with that. I tend to have fairly firm views myself which haven't varied much in the last twenty years.'

It was, however, the beginning of a period in which many old certainties were about to be shaken; in particular, public confidence in the Catholic Church was undermined by a series of scandals. In May 1992, Ireland was rocked by the revelations that the Bishop of Galway, Eamon Casey, was the father of a teenage boy and that he had financed some of his payments to the boy's American mother from diocesan funds. A few weeks after the scandal broke, Brian sat for his first set of law exams in early summer, and passed with second-class honours.

ON 30 January 1992, Charles Haughey announced his retirement from politics. His successor was Albert Reynolds, Minister for Finance in the Fianna Fáil–Progressive Democrat coalition which had been in government since 1989. The new Taoiseach, who took office that February, surprised many people when he declared that his political priority would be to bring peace to Northern Ireland.

Before the end of the year, the Fianna Fáil–Progressive Democrat coalition split when the Progressive Democrats withdrew from government, and Albert Reynold's minority Fianna

Fáil administration was subsequently defeated on a confidence motion in the Dáil. Reynolds called a general election for 25 November. With Labour more than doubling its share of the national vote in that election, speculation was that the new government would be comprised of a 'rainbow coalition', but early in the new year Fianna Fáil and Labour formed a government with Albert Reynolds as Taoiseach. The new coalition had an overall majority of thirty-six seats – the largest in Irish political history.

Albert Reynolds had only crossed the portals of Leinster House in 1977, but he had known Flor Crowley for a long time before that through his involvement in the party organisation. Reynolds had a lot in common with his Fianna Fáil colleague; both men were poker-players and non-drinkers, and they enjoyed going to race meetings. The former Taoiseach's association with the West Cork family goes back twenty-five years or more, and the bond of friendship has passed on to the second generation. The two families are close: they attend each other's weddings.

Brian was at home in Bandon, in his second year of legal studies, when he got a phone call from the new Taoiseach. 'I want you to be one of my nominees to the Senate,' Albert Reynolds told him. 'Come up to Dublin and see me.'

Brian didn't believe it at first. He thought someone was pulling his leg until the voice at the other end of the line convinced him it was indeed Albert Reynolds. But though he was shocked to be nominated to the Senate, there was never any doubt in his mind that he wanted the job.

The next day, Brian travelled to Dublin to meet the Taoiseach in his office. Reynolds explained that the reason for his appointment was that he was to use the voice he was being given in the Senate to speak up for people who did not have a voice, and to speak particularly for disabled people. Reynolds also stressed that he shouldn't change his personality, that he shouldn't change what he was. Later, Flor Crowley asked the Taoiseach if he thought Brian should cut his hair. Reynolds ruled out any scissors job. 'We have enough fecking bald men in the party,' he told Flor.

Albert Reynolds had first met Brian when he was a schoolboy attending party gatherings. Their paths crossed in Cork and Kerry in 1990 during the late Brian Lenihan's campaign for the presidency. Reynolds took an interest in Brian's progress after the accident and admired the way he didn't let his disability get on top of him.

'I used to see him occasionally at race meetings with Flor,' Albert Reynolds relates. 'We'd speak occasionally about various issues. When I had the opportunity to search around for people for the Senate, I thought about him because he could fulfil many roles in the Seanad as I saw him. First of all, he was a very pleasant person, a very intelligent young fellow, a guy with intelligence and conviction. Here was a guy in the prime of his youth who had met with this adversity, and while many people might be inclined to lie back or write off their future life, he got a new injection of life.

'I thought he would be a glorious example to the youth of the country for a start,' Reynolds continues expansively, 'and, secondly, to those with disability. In Brian, I could make a nomination to the Senate that could represent both. That was the way it was perceived in the end. I felt he had a great contribution to make, and he had a feeling for politics.'

As the first disabled person to be appointed to the Senate, his appointment made headlines, and paved the way for greater accessibility to both houses of the Oireachtas. The alterations to the building caught the imagination of the members and highlighted in a very real way the question of access for the disabled in other public buildings and in society in general. Senator David Norris remarks on how politicians had been 'bleating' for years about the need for greater accessibility for the disabled and how quickly it actually came about when Brian became senator.

The first day he went to Dublin, Brian met Eamon O'Donoghue, who had responsibility for adapting the Oireachtas for wheelchair use. He toured the building with him and architect Liam Egan, suggesting other changes that might be made. The preliminary work was done in a week. The modifications included raising floor levels to eliminate steps, widening toilet doors and providing ramps at the front entrance. Further work has been completed since then, such as putting in extra stairs lifts.

The Senate chamber itself did not require any changes except the removal of one chair. Seating arrangements in the chamber were such that Brian found himself placed beside Senator Gordon Wilson, who came to national prominence as a result of the depth of tolerance and forgiveness he displayed after he had lost his daughter, Marie, in an IRA explosion in Enniskillen, County Fermanagh, in November 1987. Brian remembers him as 'a phenomenal man'.

Very much an unknown quantity to the staff when he arrived in the Senate, Brian soon became a familiar figure in the Fianna Fáil press office on the fifth floor of Leinster House. He relied on the staff to some degree for writing speeches, but he had his own ideas and spoke beforehand to Fianna Fáil's press officer Martin Mackin about the points he wanted to make. He didn't rely very heavily on the script and he would deviate from it, making off-the-cuff remarks and observations. He took his brief extremely seriously and put in a lot of groundwork, poring over law commission reports, conscientiously researching his subjects.

Two weeks after his appointment to the Senate, Brian was made Fianna Fáil spokesman on justice and law reform. It was a dynamic portfolio, as Justice Minister Maire Geoghegan-Quinn was updating a considerable body of legislation, including the new public order bill, of which some provisions were quite contentious as regards civil liberties. The most controversial aspect of the bill was the extra powers it gave the gardaí to disperse groups of people from public areas. 'The bill allowed the guards to move on groups of people who were making trouble or causing noise,' Brian says. 'There was a fear at the time that this legislation would be used to stop people from protesting, that it would be misused.' He had misgivings about the public order act at first for this particular reason. It was discussed at party level, with the minister, with the gardaí and with residents' groups, and his eventual decision to support the bill was influenced by people he visited in areas of Dublin and Cork. Already he was settling into the role of public representative.

'The single biggest problem these people encountered on urban estates was groups of young people hanging around outside of houses, throwing bricks and banging on doors at two o'clock in the morning, and having drink parties in other people's back gardens. Elderly people in particular felt powerless and were scared to do anything about it. I took on board the concerns of people who felt trapped in their houses, and I examined if their liberties or the rights of any individuals were being affected by this law,' he says. 'I felt that people's civil rights were being infringed if they had to live with fear and harassment.' While he agreed that the solution to problems such as these takes more than just bringing in laws to detain or convict people, nonetheless, he felt that law must be put at the disposal of the gardaí to tackle crime.

Just four months after Brian Crowley took his place in the Senate, the bill decriminalising homosexuality was brought before the Oireachtas in June 1993, guaranteeing homosexuals equal treatment with heterosexuals in law. It was not the kind of measure which found favour with Brian's quite conservative values, but David Norris, a long-time campaigner for the decriminalisation of homosexuality, found him supportive on this issue nonetheless. 'He didn't talk about homosexuality, but spoke about discrimination and tolerance.'

Whatever his personal difficulties with the bill, Brian acknowledged that people's rights were being infringed by having the 1856 act on the statute books. But while he did not disagree with the act, neither did he want to see additional rights attaching to it later, such as allowing homosexual couples to marry or to adopt children. 'Whatever consenting adults want to do in privacy is their business as long as it doesn't interfere with the general good of people, and I don't think homosexuality does. But I would be concerned about the rights that grow with the progression of changing laws. An act or piece of legislation you put through does secure certain rights, but it also opens up other rights that may not be intended by the original act.'

His tone had changed, becoming more careful and deliberate to match his new role. His brief had been to be a voice for the disabled and the disadvantaged, but he bridled against having his agenda restricted. 'It was obvious that I was a disabled person. I didn't want to be categorised as one.' One of the principle things he set out to achieve was to show that the fact that he was disabled did *not* make a difference. He wanted people to focus on him, not as a disabled person, but as a senator. He wanted to speak on other matters. Initially he found it difficult to be accepted as a politician in his own right rather than as a young man in a wheelchair out to do some good. 'There was the kid gloves element towards me as there is towards all new members of the Dáil. After that, they realised I was politically motivated in other issues and other areas.'

Because he failed to maintain a single-minded focus on the issue of disability, he was criticised by disabled people who felt that he had selfishly neglected the portfolio he was given and was not being a sufficiently strong voice for the disabled, who needed someone to fight on their behalf. He acknowledges the criticism.

'A lot of the groups that represent disabled people would be very critical of me because they think I'm not radical enough or confrontational enough. I was vocal, but I was never vocal in a radical sense like marching on the street or chaining myself to the railings of Leinster House. My attitude is that it is better to be inside the gates trying to change things rather than be outside the gates just shouting and protesting.'

Among the live issues for the disabled at the time was the practice of having the Disabled Persons' Maintenance Allowance distributed by the Department of Health, rather than the Department of Social Welfare. Disabled people objected to the practice because they resented the implication that they were sick. Access to employment and educational opportunities were other important issues – eighty-nine per cent of persons with disabilities are unemployed. Brian favoured integrated education, where children with disabilities could start national school in their own area and avail of opt-out sessions during the school day for specialist education. 'Where there is integration, a five-year-old disabled child plays alongside children in their own area whom they know. This goes back to the philosophy that by educating able-bodied and disabled people together, you get rid of the prejudice.'

When Albert Reynolds established the Commission for the Status of People with Disabilities, Brian played an active part in the consultations it held with disabled people and their organisations, and he himself kept in contact with the Irish Wheelchair Association all through his time in the Senate. The commission subsequently presented a report recommending legislative changes which would favour people with disabilities. The commission, a government-appointed body, is to be followed by a council whose members will be elected by people with disabilities themselves. Crowley was also appointed as a government representative to the National Economic and Social Forum. He made contact with the Irish National Organisation for the Unemployed, the ICA, travellers' groups, the centres for the unemployed and small farmers groups, groups which could feed him information and issues they wanted raised. He was particularly impressed by the back-to-work scheme promoted by Fr Sean Healy and Brid Reynolds of CORI. The nub of the scheme was that it allowed people to work full-time while retaining their full social welfare benefits for a set period and then reducing them gradually.

Seamus Thompson, chief executive officer of the Irish Wheelchair Association, was present in Leinster House on the day Brian was appointed to the Senate. He remarks favourably on the transformation of Leinster House to accommodate wheelchair users. 'Nothing at government level has ever moved so fast. There was a lot of consultation with us and it happened very quickly. All the authorities pulled out the stops: if they hadn't done so, they were going to be highly embarrassed.' Despite differences over how best to advance the case of the disabled, Thompson believes that Brian had an 'amazing amount of success' in raising awareness of the needs and rights of the disabled. 'He helped people to recognise that physical disability just means that mobility is impaired and that the disabled can have a full and complete life.'

A great deal of the excitement surrounding Brian Crowley's appointment as a senator came simply from the fact that he himself was disabled. 'The mould was broken. You had a wheelchair representative in public life for the first time,' Seamus Thompson recalls. 'The Taoiseach was recognising that disability was something which needed to be on the agenda.' At the same time, 'Brian made it clear from very early on that he was not going to be seen as somebody with a disability. He wanted to be an all-round politician.'

Brian passed his second year exams in UCC with honours, earning him a diploma in law. In the autumn he began another two years of study with the aim of graduating with a BCL degree. He tried to keep up with his legal studies by going to college on Monday nights and having lecture notes passed on to him by his friends in the study group, but his life as a student was effectively jettisoned to make way for his new role. He wasn't allowed to fade gracefully into the upper chamber without some ribbing from his fellow students at the law faculty.

'The leather jacket gave him unending service right up to the Senate,' Dermot Clancy remarks. 'After that, I used to see the occasional suit, and then the quality of the suits improved and the jacket faded away altogether.'

His appointment was viewed by many students as a prime example of parish pump politics. Dermot Clancy again: 'He was from a family that was well-in. Everybody knew Brian's father's history. The perception was that you were lifting this guy, who used to sit up at the front in a leather jacket, and depositing him for no apparent reason into politics, into the Senate. It was a perception in certain quarters. In my own opinion, and my opinion may be biased because I'm a friend of Brian's, I think people would now see merit which perhaps Albert Reynolds saw at the time.'

The juggling act between being student and senator began on Mondays when Brian carried out constituency work during the day and attended his lectures that night before driving on to Dublin. The Senate sat from Tuesday through to Thursday. He returned home on Thursday night and the weekends were largely taken up with constituency work. He was following the politician's routine, unchanged from when he had waited on the railway station platform for his father to return from the Dáil.

Despite being immersed in this hectic routine, there was time occasionally to pick up some of the threads of his old life in the music world and to maintain some semblance of a social life. He knew a good many people in the city, guys he knew from the music business and friends from school. He knew Jon Kenny and Pat Shortt who were making waves as a comic duo, D'Unbelievables, and he went to live gigs at Bad Bobs or the Purty Loft, and occasionally to concerts like Eric Clapton, Annie

Lennox and Dave Stewart. As well as bringing Brian a new lifestyle – his base in the city was the Burlington Hotel – the Senate brought with it a steady income. He was making over £17,000 when he took office in February 1993 – a sum it would take a good few gigs to realise – and this had increased to £19,000 in April 1994. He wasn't overwhelmed by the amount. 'I believe politicians are underpaid, and not just because I am one.'

Though the Senate is regularly dismissed as a debating chamber without real political authority, Brian Crowley found that it offered a standard of discussion which was far superior to the political set pieces found in the Dáil. While Brian admired the quality of oratory in the house, his own style of delivery was considered as less than inspirational by some. One journalist, reporting from the Senate, found most of what he said 'fairly bland' and felt that he was just following the party line. However, others, such as David Norris, admired his ad lib approach to speeches and the sense of life that he conveyed. 'He spoke from the heart and with a sense of humour. He was an excellent addition to the Senate. He contributed well.' For Norris, a senator with views markedly different from Brian's, Crowley represented 'the decent side of Fianna Fáil'.

When he spoke about Northern Ireland, in particular, Brian spoke with great conviction and sincerity. He paid particular attention to the debates on the north and his republican views were tempered by the moderate unionist perspective of members such as Gordon Wilson. 'It was never rabid republicanism nor rabid unionism,' Brian recalls. 'It was controlled, logical, historical debate. I learned a lot about northern politics from other points of view.' He admired the knowledge and breadth of experience displayed by several senators, but if the debates broadened his understanding of the difficulties which needed to be overcome on the way to finding a solution to the northern problem, they did not change his opinion that a united Ireland

113

'would be better for all of us, and that there would be better protection of the rights of individuals as well as of groups in a
united Ireland'.

The times were not especially favourable for those espousing a
republican perspective. The IRA had intensified its bombing
campaign in Britain, and in October 1992 two bombs had
exploded in Manchester, injuring sixty-four people. The following March, a bomb attack in Warrington claimed the lives of
two young boys, and in April 1993 one man died and forty-four
people were injured in London's financial district, when an IRA
bomb wreaked devastation in the City. In the north, sectarian
hatred seemed to plummet to new depths, and the growing cata-
logue of atrocities – on the Shankill Road, at Greysteele and
Loughinisland – engendered a feeling of real despair.

Against this bleak and increasingly horrific background,
rounds of talks were continuing between the Irish and British
governments and the parties in Northern Ireland, but more fruit-
ful discussions were being held between SDLP leader John
Hume and Sinn Féin leader Gerry Adams. The two men main-
tained a process of dialogue throughout this period, despite the
most virulent attacks from critics north and south of the border,
and in April 1993 they offered the substance of their agreement
as a basis for negotiating a settlement in Northern Ireland. The
Hume-Adams talks brought the search for a formula to restore
stability and peace to the north into a new phase, one which
Taoiseach Albert Reynolds capitalised on, despite widespread
criticism initially. Before the end of the year, however, on 15
December 1993, Reynolds and British Prime Minister John
Major signed the Downing Street Declaration, which was widely
regarded as 'an historic opportunity for peace'. Reynolds and
Major – 'the grey men' – had between them brokered a deal.
While the declaration reaffirmed 'Northern Ireland's statutory
constitutional guarantee', the British government also stated that
it had 'no selfish strategic or economic interest in Northern

Ireland', and allowed that a united Ireland could be brought into being with the consent of the people of Ireland, north and south.

Brian was in the Fianna Fáil parliamentary rooms on the fifth floor of Leinster House when a copy of the declaration was faxed from London. He listened as Brian Lenihan delivered a speech to a packed house and the members took in these remarkable events. Just being there gave him a sense of participating in one of the historic moments of Irish political life.

By this time, some remarkable changes were also in the offing for Brian Crowley, cutting short his career as a senator. Appointed in February 1993, he handed in his resignation in July 1994. His departure from the Senate owed everything to the man who had placed him there in the first instance. Convinced from his performance that Brian Crowley's star was on the ascent, Albert Reynolds, the racegoer and the poker player, had taken a gamble on his suitability to play a role in a brighter corner of the political galaxy.

Chapter Eight

IN EARLY DECEMBER 1993, Albert Reynolds got on the phone to Brian Crowley once again. Would Brian consider going before Fianna Fáil's January convention to try for selection as one of their candidates in the European elections? Brian told Reynolds he would not even consider it. He was really taken aback. Being a senator was more than he had hoped to achieve, and it seemed to him far too soon to be thinking in terms of becoming an MEP. He simply didn't think he was qualified. Reynolds responded by saying that he thought Brian was ideal for the job and that he didn't need an immediate answer. 'Think about it for a week or two,' he told Brian. 'Discuss it with the family and see what they think.'

Fianna Fáil was in need of new blood for the European elections which were to be held the following summer. The party was in a difficult situation because the number of seats in the Munster region had been reduced from five to four, but even so, Reynolds was taking a huge gamble in parachuting a virtual unknown into a campaign race that would turn out to be top-heavy with personalities.

Unlike a Dáil election, which can be fought in a snap campaign of three to four weeks, a European election is a long drawn-out affair. The demands on Euro candidates are far greater as they must canvass a whole province rather than a section of a county. Munster alone covers thirteen Dáil constituencies and includes two of the country's largest cities, Cork and Limerick. It was seen as one of the toughest and tightest constituencies in the 1994 European election. The loss of a fifth seat because of a decline in population was an important factor; candidates would have about 100,000 fewer votes to take into consideration than in the previous European election in 1989. There was also the question of what would be the fate of over 50,000 votes which had previously gone to the outgoing Independent MEP, TJ Maher, who was retiring.

A week or two before Christmas, Brian told his brother Niall about Reynold's request. What did he think? Niall was pessimistic. As a marketing graduate, he knew how difficult it was to launch any new product on to the market, and as the son of a former TD he was well aware of the pitfalls of the political marketplace, particularly in relation to financial costs. He put it to Brian that surely he was aware that there was a question mark over whether Fianna Fáil would actually manage to hold on to its two seats in Munster, and that if he did go forward he would be running against Gerard Collins, one of the party's most experienced politicians and a consistent poll-topper. Anyway, he needed the support of at least thirty *cumainn*, and the other candidates had already started canvassing the support of delegates. The convention was in January and it was now December, surely too late to start looking for support.

A few days after Christmas, Brian rang Albert Reynolds back. Thanks but no, he wouldn't go forward, he said, and he listed out his reasons. Reynolds agreed, yes, he was new, yes, it was very late, yes, he was up against Gerard Collins, but he reckoned that if they got a good team behind him, Brian was in with a chance. And anyway he had a gut feeling about this; he figured they could do it. Go for it, he persisted. Brian decided there and then to make the pitch for Europe.

There is no question that Brian Crowley was very late in terms of eliciting support from *cumann* delegates for the convention.

With many of the *cumainn* in Munster having already decided how they were going to vote, it was a question of looking for party branches' second or third preferences after their first-choice candidate had been selected. Brian and Niall began making phone calls. They rang as many delegates as possible and Brian began driving around Munster attending *comhairle* meetings and asking *cumann* secretaries to nominate him. This frequently involved going in cold to meetings, knowing no one and trying to sell himself. He had two main advantages, however: he could use some of his father's contacts to open doors and he knew all the sitting TDs through meeting them on a daily basis in Leinster House.

The most intriguing aspect of the denouement of any electoral campaign under the proportional representation system is the fact that the opponents facing each other are often from the same parties. This makes the political contest an internal one. It means that rivalry in a campaign is between members of the same party if three candidates from the same party (as happened in the 1994 elections) are primed for two seats. Nowhere is this more evident than at convention level where daggers are drawn as candidates vie for party selection. Efforts to block candidates and prevent their securing nominations are common. At the January convention, a rival faction's attempt to block a fellow candidate was to work to Brian Crowley's advantage.

The convention was held on 23 January in Cork's City Hall, where Brian took up a prominent position in the middle of the foyer, directly in the path of all the incoming delegates. However, enthusiastic though he might have been, Brian's tardy start hadn't impressed the seasoned party members, and when the results of the first count were announced, he had secured only fifty-three votes out of a potential 1,000. As expected, Gerard Collins had topped the poll on the first count with 439 votes, followed by Paddy Lane with 215. Expectations were that it would be these two candidates who were sure of selection.

Before the first count, however, Brian had spotted an attempt to block Paddy Lane. He told Lane that he would ask his supporters to give him second preference on the next round of votes, and asked him to return the favour. After Paddy Lane was elected, it came down to a vote between Tom Coughlan and Brian to decide who would take the remaining position. With the help of votes from Lane's supporters, and to the astonishment of convention delegates, Brian Crowley secured the nomination to campaign for a seat in the European parliament.

Reporting in the *Sunday Business Post* afterwards, Frank Connolly described the convention as 'tense and contentious'. He commented that it was 'to the dismay' of the other camps that Crowley was receiving such public support from senior party members. Quizzed on *Questions and Answers* towards the end of the campaign, Brian was asked what he thought of Gerard Collins' alleged description of the Cork convention as a 'fiasco'. He answered that he had thought the convention 'very exciting, very democratic' and 'a bit like Lester Piggott in the Grand National'. However, despite Crowley's lack of gravity, there was a general awareness throughout the campaign that the rivalry between Crowley and Collins on the regional level reflected rivalry on a national level, with party leader Albert Reynold's supporters backing Crowley and ousted leader Charles Haughey's backing Collins.

PAT Fenton had only just begun to explain the kind of work he wanted done to the central heating when the 'tradesman' began talking about the European elections. Pat and his caller were at cross-purposes: it wasn't Brian Crowley the plumber who had rung but Brian Crowley the politician. Brian wanted to know if Fenton would help with his campaign for Europe. Would he set up a strategy team for the campaign? Fenton was surprised at the request, but agreed to meet Niall who, despite his initial reservations, had agreed to act as Brian's campaign director.

Joining the old Munster and Leinster Bank in Cork in 1956, Pat Fenton was based for the next thirty-seven years in the South Mall where he served as senior manager, company secretary and manager of AIB's credit card services in the south of Ireland. But there were other sides to the banker's life. For almost twenty years he had been involved in the theatre on a semi-professional basis as player, producer and director. And if the theatre didn't provide him with enough burlesque, Pat Fenton also had the political life of the city to draw on. The longest-standing member of the Fianna Fáil finance committee in Cork city, he was highly respected for his organisational skills. It was these skills which prompted the invitation to him to join Brian Crowley's campaign.

A week later he met Niall in the Rochestown Park hotel in Cork. The marketing graduate presented him with 'a very optimistic scenario'. Pat Fenton remembers Niall's sales pitch: 'He seemed to indicate that Brian was going to take the first place and we had at least half a million pounds in finance.' Fenton asked a lot of questions and listened carefully. He was not convinced. He concluded, rather, that Brian Crowley had absolutely no prospect of being elected to Europe. 'I frankly didn't believe that he'd be elected.' However, he decided to give it a shot. His decision to throw his lot behind Brian Crowley's election campaign and set up a strategy team was influenced largely by the fact that he had just retired from banking and could see a 'little window of time' opening up. He opted to use it on the campaign. 'There was no specific trigger,' he recalls. 'Just me saying, "We'll meet a few friends, have a bit of fun along the way. And at the end of it, we'll have an interesting wake when he doesn't get the seat."'

Fenton wasn't enthusiastic at the prospect of chairing the strategy team himself, but his experience in the past had made him all too aware of the weakness of committees where 'everybody's responsibility is nobody's responsibility'. He felt it essential to allocate areas of responsibility immediately and set about placing a structure on the team. The main concern, however, was the hole that he saw in the financial net. Money was needed if there was to be any hope of winning a seat and raising it was thus an immediate priority. From his own experience of raising money for Fianna Fáil, he knew how difficult the task could be.

The strategy team was made up of people who 'gelled well together'. Among the early recruits were Michael Doody, a solicitor in Cork city, and Michael's wife, Cathy, personal friends of Pat Fenton's. Gerry Byrne, who was chairman of the Dáil Ceantar at the time and Pat Power, both from Cork TD Batt O'Keeffe's camp, were also conscripts. Also in the ranks were Michael Martin's right-hand man, Humphrey Murphy, Kieran Coleman from former TD John Dennehy's camp, advertising executive Manus O'Callaghan and Bandon accountant Niall O'Driscoll. Local Fianna Fáil activist and publican Con Dennehy came on board, followed by accountant Sean O'Riordan, Sean Casey and Eddie O'Connor, and Dr Kevin James, from Cork Regional Technical College, who eventually ran the polls for the campaign. And three men – John Hodnett, Ray O'Mahony and 'Curly' Cahalane – who had worked for Flor in previous years, now became his son's 'kitchen cabinet'.

One notable absence from the team was Flor Crowley himself. There were whispers outside the Crowley camp that Flor had been 'housed' for the duration because of his political falling-out in West Cork and a fear that they might lose Fianna Fáil votes as a result. Brian Crowley denies that this was the reason he didn't sit in on the core team. He says that the main reason was because of his health: 'He didn't have the physical endurance to be all the time campaigning because of his heart. He couldn't take that type of pressure.' Yet while Flor senior might not have been part of Brian's public campaign, behind the scenes he was busy canvassing support from old comrades.

A CHIEF difference between Dáil and European elections is that personalities loom larger in the European arena. There is a sense that candidates are being chosen to represent the country rather than to form a government. The 1994 campaign was top heavy with personalities in Munster. Brian Crowley's running partners on the Fianna Fáil ticket were Paddy Lane and Gerard Collins. Fine Gael was fielding the UCC professor of agriculture Tom Raftery and MEP John Cushnahan. Labour TD Jim Kemmy was contesting the European election for the first time, and another Limerick man, Progressive Democrats founder Des O'Malley was also on his first European outing.

Limerick was also to see the emergence of Independent candidate Nora Bennis, who was to gain national prominence as one of the founding members of a new political grouping, Family Solidarity. Democratic Left's bid for entry to Brussels was in the hands of Kathleen Lynch, a member of Cork Corporation, and the Green party entered the fray with Dan Boyle. And in April, a surprise candidate entered into the running, Progressive Democrat TD and MEP Pat Cox, who would turn out to be Brian's most significant non-party rival. Both were young and attractive, and were perceived to draw the same type of voter, women in particular. Cox, who broke ranks with the PDs to run in the elections as an Independent candidate and against his former party leader Des O'Malley, had received 85,558 first preference votes in the 1989 European elections and gained 17.3 per cent of the Munster vote in all.

As the candidates lined up at the start, Brian's strategy team set about putting a campaign together and deciding on a strategy. Pat Fenton and Niall met almost every morning and the team met originally once a week and, later on in the campaign, twice a week. A decision was made at the outset that the team would act independently of Brian. In fact, Crowley was to attend only three strategy meetings in all – at the beginning, middle and end of the campaign – for two main reasons: firstly, it was felt that

Brian's place was out canvassing and meeting the electorate, not at meetings; and secondly, it was recognised that his presence might be intimidatory. 'Team members,' Pat Fenton said, 'would be constantly looking to him for approval.' The move gave the team the freedom to plan strategy for Brian unhindered. 'He did everything suggested by Niall, the campaign manager, without question.'

The first priority for the team was fundraising. Where was the money going to come from? There were a variety of sources. The first was Brian himself. He went to the banks and got clearance for two loans at two different banks for £70,000. The rest of the fund-raising was in the hands of the strategy committee.

Brian was lucky in that he could rely on well-wishers to help raise money. Two hundred people attended a 'Brendan Grace Lunch' at the Imperial Hotel in Cork. Ex-European commissioner and Fianna Fáil veteran Ray McSharry helped to raise over £5,000 by his attendance at a £50-a-head dinner in Cork and by appearing as a guest speaker at a business lunch. One of the most successful money-spinners of the campaign was a Buddy Holly Night in the Cork Opera House where tickets were bought for £100 per couple. Individual team-members also did their bit: Pat Fenton brought in a 'dowry' of £7,000 from a dance he had organised with the Central Finance Committee in Cork city.

Advertising turned out to be one of the highest costs of the team's budget. One of the most expensive items in the advertising budget of over £35,000 was the production of 250,000 copies of a glossy four-page colour brochure and its delivery by An Post, which cost £20,000. Careful media planning was in evidence from the start. Coming from an advertising background, Manus O'Callaghan was the driving force behind the slick and professional advertising strategy. An early move was the block-booking of advertising slots right up to the eve of the election. These included prime front-page slots in the *Cork*

Examiner and provincial newspapers and full billboard posters of Brian around the province. This would reap dividends throughout the campaign.

No mention was made of Brian's disability in the media campaign. According to Con Dennehy, the reason for this was that the team felt that 'It would have backfired if we went out and played on the wheelchair, that he was a "poor fellow who needed a job and he's intelligent enough so we'll send him to Europe". People would have rejected that. He's too good for that.' Manus O'Callaghan explains how it was also a deliberate marketing strategy not to use the wheelchair in the advertising campaign. 'In the advertising business, we look for unique selling points, and Brian's major point of difference for the general public was the wheelchair,' he says. But in his initial brief, Niall Crowley had asked Manus to consider Brian's 'young, attractive face and unusual long hair' as a selling point rather than the chair. This set the tone and mood of the campaign – the wheelchair was never shown or talked about in the advertising. The public discovered this aspect of the candidate by themselves, and facts that you discover by yourself are somehow more memorable.

The electorate were beginning to recognise Brian from seeing his face on billboards and newspaper photographs, but now the main objective was to get Brian to meet the people. One of the first things the team did was draw up a list of everything that was happening in Munster leading up to the elections, from marts and fair days to festivals and football matches. The team's view was that if Brian could meet everybody in Munster on a one-to-one basis, everybody he met would vote for him. They decided to try something that had never been done for a European election before; they decided to send Brian door-to-door.

ANOTHER housing estate, another doorstep. Brian rings the bell and waits for someone to answer. The man puts his hand in his pocket, but Brian shakes his head: 'No, sir, I'm not collecting for the Wheelchair Society. I'm looking for your vote in the European election.' A morning in a poverty-stricken suburb of Cork's northside highlights the charisma Brian Crowley has in dealing with people. In Knocknaheeny, a sprawling unemployment blackspot of over two thousand homes and few amenities, one shopping centre, one church and one pub, Brian received an 'incredible' reception. The connection Crowley made with people on the canvass trail was obvious. Flor senior remarks with a laugh, 'They were queuing up to meet him. Anytime I stood in an election, they were running away from me.'

There was a lot of road to cover in Munster during the campaign. Along the way, Brian clocked up 47,000 miles, wore out four sets of tyres in the wheelchair and about three sets in the car. 'I survived with five or six hours of sleep,' he relates. The mornings were spent driving to venues to canvass, the evenings at Fianna Fáil functions or meetings where the focus was on building up contacts within the organisation and trying to get members on side and willing to canvass for him.

Brian may have had a very difficult mountain to scale, but from very early on in the campaign he had his eyes firmly fixed on the summit. 'I honestly believed from the start when I got selected that I was going to win,' he says. 'I never said it to anybody. Well, I did say it to my father one day. I think it was Patrick's Day and we were in Sneem canvassing. We came back home that night and Dad asked how I got on. I said it was tough enough. He asked how I thought I would do, and I said, "Don't say it to anybody, but I think I'm going to head the poll." He said he felt the same. Neither of us said it to anybody and we never spoke about it again.'

The atmosphere of the campaign, which had begun in the cold of winter, changed perceptibly as momentum picked up and the months slipped by to bring warmer days and brighter evenings. But it was to be a summer of sunshine and horror, a season forever haunted by the murder of a priest, a mother and her young son in a Clare woodland. South Africa held its first democratic elections in April. In May, the western world mourned the loss of an icon with the death of Jacqueline Kennedy. From Africa came stories of Rwanda's killing fields. And somewhere in the middle of all this, candidates in the European election sought to snatch valuable column inches in newspapers to publicise a contest that the vast majority of voters, with the notable exception of farmers, had scant interest in.

Bemused GAA fans on their way into the match are smiling at the crowd singing at the tops of their voices in the pouring rain. A few of the fans step out of the passing blur of colour to swing around and dance with the girls in their Brian Crowley tee-shirts. The football fans are treated to a change of spectacle when two rows of Pat Cox's canvassers decide to walk through the Crowley team, who start shouting 'Crowley, Crowley, Crowley' and dancing exuberantly to the strains of 'Eye of the Tiger' and other songs played out of their van. The tape runs out and the chant changes to 'We're the Crowleys', with Flor junior adding, 'I've got all my sisters with me!'

For many motorists making their way sleepily to work in the mornings, the lasting image of the Euro campaign 1994 will be of clean-cut young men and women lining Cork roundabouts in Brian Crowley tee-shirts. Strategy team member Sean O'Riordan had come up with idea for a 'youth team' who would maintain a presence at matches, churches, roundabouts and shopping-centres in the run-up to the election. This was possibly the most attention-grabbing feature of the Crowley campaign.

The youth team was based in Sally Crowley's old home, Avoca, on the Wilton Road where they met every morning before the canvassing began. A canvass could start as early as 7.45 am to catch the early-morning commuters. Afterwards, they came back to Avoca for breakfast and a browse through the papers. The group consisted of about fifteen young people (the eldest member was twenty-five). There was a mixture of Ógra Fianna Fáil, friends of the family, students, workers and unemployed people. Nineteen-year-old Susan Conway was the youngest member of the team. 'Brian was the uniting factor,' she relates. 'We were there for Brian, supporting him not alone in his political ambitions or his party ambitions, but for his own ambitions for himself.' She had been doing a part-time course in public relations and working in Roches Stores when one of her friends, who was very active in Fianna Fáil, asked her to join the campaign. One of the things that impressed her about Brian was his interest in all the team members. She tells how he made a special effort to get to know her when she joined the team first. After canvassing in Bantry, Brian asked that she travel with him so that they could chat on the way back to the city. 'It wasn't heavy political talk. It was more, "Are you enjoying yourself; are you getting to know people?"'

Brian Crowley wasn't just lucky that he had a great team behind him, he was lucky also in that key Fianna Fáil TDs such as Batt O'Keeffe, Michael Martin, Michael Ahern, Danny Wallace and Brendan Kenneally came to the fore and mobilised their people in support of his campaign. It was the first time that key members of opposing Fianna Fáil camps in Cork city had united to work together for a common cause. 'An unusual feeling in Fianna Fáil,' one member noted.

But while Brian had an uncommonly united party machine behind him, it was clear that it would take more than Fianna Fáil muscle to edge their candidate across the finishing line. Because of this, a decision was taken at the very outset of the campaign to cast the net far wider than seasoned Fianna Fáil campaigners to include, in a very unusual step, people with no political allegiance. Niall Crowley explains: 'A lot of candidates would run on their own selected core teams, but we tried to involve as many people as possible. A lot were people who were politically involved recently and people who weren't. The gelling of that was quite successful. You need the people with political noses, but you also need the people who are not blinkered into thinking in a particular way.'

While Niall came from a political family, he had not been actively involved in the party. His particular expertise lay in his management and motivation skills. The other member of the strategy team who made a singularly non-political contribution was Manus O'Callaghan.

Manus O'Callaghan is the type of man you dread to meet at school reunions, especially if you've been slouching through life at a handy pace. Motivated and organised, he appears to have everything under control – the successful business and the nice home in the suburbs. Born in Mallow in 1948, he has worked in advertising since he was twenty-one and is currently managing director of Southern Advertising. His world is that of unique selling points and catchy slogans. Politically, he would have voted for all parties through the years, gravitating more towards Fine Gael at first, then drifting towards Fianna Fáil, the Progressive Democrats and Labour, usually pulled by particular candidates he thought were gifted in some way.

Manus recognised the 'non-political baggage' surrounding Brian Crowley and he liked that. All the other candidates were by nature elder statesmen in the game. He thought they were 'obvious and too easy'. Brian Crowley had an air of bringing something new and fresh on the scene. Manus felt it was a bit like Mary Robinson's impact in the presidential election, where a candidate with a difference could make a difference to an office commonly regarded as a retirement ground for old men. Manus O'Callaghan brought on board the expertise that other campaigns were buying in from outside. The difference in the Crowley strategy was that with them he worked as an insider.

SHE was a woman of indeterminate age, but certainly a woman who should have had more sense than to be caught red-handed making off with her trophy on the side of the main road to Bantry. Caught by Brian's campaign team in the act of carefully removing a 'Brian Crowley' poster from a pole, she helped solve one of the mysteries of the Crowley campaign. Why were all the posters of Brian disappearing from the campaign trail? It was put down to rivals' tactics at first, but now they were finding out that Brian's posters were starting to decorate his female fans' bedroom walls. Women of all ages take a shine to Brian Crowley, and during the European campaign he wasn't slow to capitalise on this. His sister-in-law, Adrienne, offers an explanation: 'The older ones want to mother him and the younger ones want to go out with him.' Susan Conway describes an encounter with a woman who offered to buy a Brian Crowley tee-shirt for £250. 'She wanted me to give it to her there and then,' she says. 'I couldn't give it to her because I had nothing else to wear, but she asked me to post it out to her and she would send me £250.'

They made a conscious decision to target women's votes. Crowley acknowledges that he 'actively encouraged and went after women voters, because from a practical point of view, they are fifty-one per cent of the population'. As part of his campaign, he set up meetings with women's groups in different areas. His aunt, Kathleen Doyle, organised a coffee morning in Jury's Hotel in Cork, which over three hundred women attended. The meeting was remarkable both for the high attendance and for Brian's novel approach in the campaign. He told the attendance that if each woman there went out and got him ten votes, it would mean that he would be elected. He spoke about general campaign issues and more specific issues like childcare. The questions and answers went from agricultural policy to education policy to employment and social welfare policy to the environment. Brian comments that it was 'great that it wasn't just ghettoised into one particular thing'.

But he wasn't a success with all women. 'I remember one particular meeting that I did during the campaign with a certain association,' he recalls, 'and I got a desperate doing at that because of my attitude.' The association in question was the Cork Women's Political Association, which held a conference about four weeks before polling day on the theme, 'How Women Friendly are Our European Candidates?' At the conference, Brian spoke out strongly against having a quota for the employment of women and was criticised harshly for his position. He maintains his opinion today. His argument is that quotas can reinforce discrimination. In Crowley's eyes, if you are applying for a job, you should be 'judged on your ability, not on your sex or not because you are disabled or not disabled'. His belief is that the only way true equality can be achieved is by education, and by changing attitudes. He admits openly that these views did not go down well amongst the women's group, but 'We agreed on a lot of other things.'

Neither did his views on divorce go down particularly well at a media lunch that was held in the Arbutus Lodge a week afterwards on 17 May. What was intended to be a relatively low-key affair turned into a bit of an 'argy-bargy' (as one insider termed it) when Brian was asked how he stood on divorce. Crowley answered that he was against it on the grounds that he didn't believe it worked. Brian's position that marriage is for life is in essence a religious belief. 'As a practising Catholic, I believe in the rules of my church. That is not to say I don't dispute some of them and argue them, but there is a certain Catholic belief that marriage is for life. It's part of my personality and my experience of life,' he says. He decried the lack of open debate in the run-up to the divorce referendum and claims that Fianna Fáil was the only party which had open public debate on the topic. 'What it showed more than anything else was that there were people who actually wanted to express an opinion and that politicians will always take the easy option because it's the safest road to take, but sometimes you have to get off the fence and declare yourself,' he says. 'I think there was far too much muzzling in the whole general debate.'

His stance was influenced by both his personal belief and the argument of the 'greater good'. 'I don't think divorce is for the greater good and I don't think it's the better solution,' he says. 'I honestly believe that having divorce within your legal system and within your society is actually harmful because of the knock-on effect. One of the biggest misgivings I have about it is the rights of children in a divorce. I can understand how easy it would be for two adults that were married and who have no obligations to look for a divorce and to remarry. I can see few difficulties with that, but when children become involved a whole new set of responsibilities, obligations and rights attach to that.' One of the suggestions he put forward when he saw divorce legislation going through was that children would be entitled to have a separate legal representation at all divorce hearings to put forward their point of view and to secure their rights.

Some members of the strategy team would have advised Brian to side-step the issue – it was a national question rather than a European question. 'I was one of the ones who said to him, "Leave that thing alone, don't get involved," Kevin James says. 'In fact, again, I was wrong. There was a positive response to his position on divorce, even among young people. Looking at reactions from polls and talking to people in canvassing, that was a positive thing. But also his actual stating what he believed in.'

Despite the controversy that arose in the media following Brian's acknowledgement of his anti-divorce stance, it was his handling of the media which was credited by Crowley insiders – and outsiders – for establishing him as a force to contend with. In fact, it was when Brian saw himself on the media that he became truly confident of his chances of winning a seat in Europe. RTE's *Prime Time* transmitted a pre-election special in

April, and Brian watched as a clip was shown of Labour's Dick Spring and Jim Kemmy walking into a shopping centre in Cork where Brian was canvassing. In the surprise meeting with the Labour figures, the dominant visual image is of Brian wheeling towards the camera and greeting them, with a dramatic out-stretching of both arms, with 'Welcome to Cork'. The expansive gesture and the *bonhomie* of his chat exude confidence. 'That was a key point for me because it showed me as an equal to the national figures and it showed in the public perception that I could be as good if not better,' he says. 'The crowds were with me; they weren't going to them.' And it was another media success that convinced his team that Crowley was in with a chance.

It was 23 May and a little over two weeks to election day. Brian looked uncomfortable as the camera zoomed in and John Bowman filled the studio audience in on his background. Clearly trying to hold a set expression while the presenter talked exclusively about him, his eyes glanced in different directions and there was a noticeable nervous intake of breath. He was wearing a blue shirt behind a large, colourful tie. There was a story behind the shirt: only an hour before Brian was to head to the TV studio, the team noticed that the one he was wearing had a curled-up collar and wrinkles visible beneath the tie. No way was the candidate appearing on national TV in that! 'It was dreadful,' recalls Kevin James. Michael Doody was dispatched to buy a blue shirt. (There was strategy at work here, too: apparently, in media terms, blue is 'honest'.)

The Fianna Fáiler in the blue shirt featured on the programme along with outgoing Dublin MEP Bernie Malone, Labour, former Fine Gael TD and Euro hopeful Monica Barnes and *Sunday Business Post Editor* Damien Kiberd. Whatever about the shirt's contribution to Brian's success on *Questions and Answers*, the strategy team was jubilant about his performance. Brian held his own and came across as articulate and competent. The team regarded it as an important coup that Brian had got the 'quieter slot' in Dublin where the other panellists were largely interested in the Leinster election.

'The reports we were getting back was that everywhere he went, he was making an impression,' Niall Crowley recalls. 'But he hadn't been exposed to much national profile. I knew he was good, but the difficulty I had was what opportunities was he going to get to show that prowess. A key point would have been his performance on *Questions and Answers*. It launched him from being a very saleable candidate on the ground into a candidate who suddenly made a national impact because of his performance on the night. It showed his calibre.'

The team members were ecstatic after the programme. On the journey back to Cork, mobile phones buzzed as they called up the jubilant reactions from Crowley supporters. It looked as if young Crowley was heading for Europe.

Chapter Nine

B RIAN CROWLEY WAS a rank outsider when the odds were chalked up for the European elections in February. Ever the gambler, he decided to back himself anyway to head the poll at odds of 35 to 1. He suggested to a few members of the strategy team that they should put down a collective bet, reckoning that they would cover their election costs if they won – and if they lost, well, £2,000 was hardly going to matter if the campaign was down £70,000. There were no takers, though. It was some weeks before the others took sufficient courage from the results of the polls to put their hands in their pockets, and by then the odds against a Crowley victory were very much shorter.

Kevin James had responsibility for overseeing the polls, which would help the team estimate how well Brian was doing in advance of the actual vote. Early on in the campaign, before he got down to conducting the polls proper, James had tested the water by carrying out a straw poll based on candidate recognition at his workplace. He found it disheartening: asked to name the candidates in the election, most people had been able to come up with Gerard Collins but Brian had hardly been mentioned.

However, by the time the first polls were carried out at the beginning of April, the results were much more optimistic. To avoid bias, non-party members were employed to conduct the research, middle-aged women in particular as it was felt that they were 'non-aggressive' and 'most likely to get the answer'. In shopping centres in Cork, respondents were questioned on a random basis and asked if they knew Brian Crowley, if they would vote for him, and what they thought of him. The team was stunned when the poll indicated a massive recognition factor for Crowley. The result gave him an enormous 35.6 per cent of the vote. Because the surveys were carried out in shopping centres and focused mostly on women, sceptics like Kevin James felt that they could not possibly be a true reflection of the general level of support. Nevertheless, when the area covered was widened for the next poll Crowley once more emerged as leader. The final poll, taken on 15 May was based on interviews with 800 people in forty centres throughout Munster, excluding Limerick and Clare. The Crowley team's poll and a Fine Gael survey were carried out on the same weekend. When both results were published, they showed that Brian had topped not only his own poll, but the Fine Gael one as well.

The strategy team recognised that the polls could serve a purpose other than just boosting the campaigners' confidence; they could also be used for clever media campaigning. The tactic used was what a psychologist might term 'interpolation', though media strategist Manus O'Callaghan was more inclined to call it sheer 'cop-on'. Respondents had described Crowley as young, talented and courageous, so photographs of Brian soon beamed from billboards and colour newspaper adverts headlined with these phrases and the slogan 'Time for a fresh start' or 'Time for a change'. Little wonder that they seemed familiar to the voters; they were simply repeating voters' own words.

A review of the Cork campaign in the *Sunday Business Post* on 29 May described Brian as 'one of the real shock factors' in the election. He was now just three or four percentage points behind Gerard Collins. Collins showed 16 per cent support and looked a certainty for election, but Brian at 13 per cent was starting to appear as a safe bet for the second seat. 'All parties now agree that Gerry Collins and Brian will take the first and second seats,' Niall told the paper. As the message of the polls hit home, those who had earlier resisted the impulse to place a few greenbacks with the bookie finally threw caution to the wind.

The sun was streaming through the open window of the car as Brian drove down to the Town Hall in Bandon on the morning of Thursday, 9 June, to cast his vote. He posed at the ballot box for the photographers, then called to a few of the polling stations around West Cork before taking time out for a separate mission. During the course of campaigning, he had met a family whose daughter had special learning needs. Her twenty-first birthday coincided with polling day, and with a bunch of flowers and a present in the back seat of the car, he drove to the hillside farm outside Bandon to wish her a happy birthday.

Two days later, the tallymen and party supporters were wedged shoulder to shoulder in the count centre, watching like hawks as the voting papers were spilled out of the boxes and onto the benches for counting. There was exhilaration in the Crowley camp as box after box confirmed what the polls had been forecasting. Brian was elated. He looked set to take the seat with a sweeping majority. As high as his spirits soared, he tried to hold them in check. After all, these were just the tallies, and though the tallymen were experienced and accurate, it was the final, official announcement that would seal his success.

Brian got up around lunchtime on the day the results were to be announced. There was nothing more he could do and he needed a sleep-in after the months of campaigning. Family and supporters went with him to the Neptune Stadium in Cork's northside to hear the official results. The stadium is usually crammed with screaming basketball fans, but on Sunday, 12 June, it was full of waiting Euro hopefuls and their supporters.

There is an anxious silence as returning officer W. F. O'Connor takes to the floor. He announces that Brian Crowley has been elected to the European parliament on the first count with a total of 84,463 votes. As his supporters erupt all round him, Brian smiles broadly and gives the thumbs up, then shakes the hands of those reaching in from the crowd. Traditionally, a successful candidate is hoisted shoulder high by supporters; today the Crowley camp content themselves with breaking into the World Cup chant, 'Olé, Olé, Olé'. His arms, stretching to reach the many hands straining to touch his, look perilously close to being wrenched from their sockets.

Brian Crowley is 'the real story of the election', says RTE reporter Tom McSweeney from the stadium. He has managed to come from nowhere to displace some of the biggest names in Irish politics. He has romped home with the best first-preference vote ever in a European election in Ireland, and he is also the first Fianna Fáil candidate for Europe to get in on the first count. As Brian turns to speak to the cameras his face is glowing, his freckles reflecting the sunny weeks on the campaign trail.

That evening, euphoric supporters crowded into the ballroom at Jury's Hotel for the mother of all parties. There were speeches from Brian and from his father and from party members, and then Brian sat in to the piano. Carried by the elation of the day, he sang and played into the early hours of the morning. It was broad daylight before the last of the revellers left the ballroom.

As predicted, the second Fianna Fáil seat in Munster went to Gerard Collins while John Cushnahan and Pat Cox took the third and fourth seats. How did Gerard Collins feel about being displaced as a consistent poll-topper for over thirty years? In a post-election TV special he pointed out that Cork city and county accounted for about 40 per cent of the entire electorate in the Munster constituency, and this was Brian's 'area'. Collins also commented that a lot of money had been spent on the Crowley campaign, adding that his own budget had been 'very limited'. He attributed the great difficulty he had in raising money to his coming from a rural constituency. But can Crowley's success be put down entirely to skilled fundraising? Any analysis indicates that a variety of factors contributed to his extraordinary result in the European election.

His youth helped: half of Ireland's population is under twenty-five and Crowley was only thirty when he took the seat. With long hair and a bubbly personality, he was a breath of fresh air on the political scene. Crowley was also a 'clean' candidate: he carried no legacy of having made wrong decisions and he was too new to the political scene to have made enemies.

Another component in Brian's success was his ability to cross the party divide. Crowley managed to strike a chord that rose above party logos, and voters responded accordingly.

His family background would not have been a hindrance. Brian 'had a degree in politics from the house he came from,' Dan Joe O'Mahony quipped.

'There was never any "God help us" with him – ever. And he proved it. The minute he got any kind of a platform at all, he was away on a hack. He scored all the time because he has great charisma, tremendous ability. And he had the old breeding, the father's *grá mo chroí* and the grandfather's. 'Twas all there. It all helped, that's what did it.'

Appointing his brother as director of elections was the icing on the cake. With his management skills, Niall was credited with being one of the main motivators in the strategy team. Totally dedicated to his brother, emotionally as much as politically, he insisted on the best throughout the campaign. Some ask why it was Brian and not Niall who went into politics.

'Brian really was the only one in the family interested in politics,' Niall says. 'I didn't think about it ever. The difference between a politician's life and the way the public perceive it to be is vast and unreal. Even now, there is a stigma attached to being a politician. Absolute total commitment before everything else is required. I just wouldn't have the patience or the tolerance to go through clinics, dinners, meetings. I wouldn't be prepared to give up that much of my personal life for it. Anyone who is doing well in a career would take a major drop in disposable income going into politics... If you're running a business and you work hard and are committed, it's unlikely anything will go wrong whereas in politics, anything can happen. One misplaced statement can virtually ruin you.' Yet while he may not have been gripped by an addiction to politics, it is accepted by almost all political pundits that Niall was one of the biggest factors in his brother's extraordinary success.

Family connections with senior members of the party was certainly a point in Brian Crowley's favour. One front page ad in the *Cork Examiner* featured Brian with Albert Reynolds and MEP Gene Fitzgerald under the heading 'The Winning Team for Cork'. Brian agrees that many senior party members helped him out because of personal friendships with his father. Political rivalry played a part also. Crowley was regarded as the Reynolds' candidate set to run against 'Haughey's man', Gerard Collins. Reynolds had earlier dropped Collins from government and, as one one Fianna Fáil source suggested at the time, 'if Collins does well, it will be one in the eye to Reynolds, and that is what Collins wants to achieve'.

Did his disability help? Did the electorate turn out for him in such numbers because of his wheelchair? Brian himself feels that if the sympathy factor did have a bearing, it would account for no more than 2 per cent of his vote. Flor Crowley discounts sympathy as a relevant factor. He recalls an answer Galway MEP Mark Killilea gave to someone who had suggested that a certain politician's widow would get the sympathy vote in a by-election. 'He said, "She will indeed. The only place she'll find sympathy in Ireland is between sin and syphilis in the dictionary."'

Crowley also had an excellent team behind him. The strategy team committed themselves fully to the campaign, working behind the scenes to ensure that the candidate was free to meet the voters, while the youth team made sure that Crowley was always in the public's mind with their high-profile campaigning around the constituency. Of course, none of this would have been possible without strong financial backing. A combination of fundraising and donations from private sources ensured that the Crowley campaign team was able to use resources imaginatively and effectively to launch a virtual unknown into European politics.

Brian Crowley's own analysis of his success is to the point and sparing: 'First, canvassing got me there; second, television; third, the image factor – being young, different, fresh; and fourth was the political connections.'

BRIAN Crowley wheels across the tarmac to the plane. It is Monday morning in Cork Airport, the beginning of his journey to Brussels. As the rest of the passengers walk up the aircraft steps, Brian goes to the rear of the plane where he is raised to the aircraft's door by a forklift truck. Once aboard he transfers into a wheelchair small enough to pass through the aisle. The 7.50 a.m. flight from Cork is destined for Heathrow where he is to catch the 10.30 a.m. connection to Brussels. At Heathrow, boarding the Brussels flight presents no complications because of the airbridge facility. Brian scans the newspapers. The seat beside him is free, so he stretches out to sleep.

The European parliament migrates between Brussels and Strasbourg. Strasbourg is the edge of the world in commuting terms and seems to take forever to reach. In summer, Brian might fly from Cork to Strasbourg via Paris; in winter, the route can be via Brussels or Amsterdam by air or from Frankfurt by car. When he was first elected, the Strasbourg trip was taking as much as eleven or twelve hours, most of the time spent hanging around airports: 'If you could literally get off one plane and get immediately onto another, it would be fantastic. But there are always delays – if the flight goes wrong, if there's fog.' Within twelve months, travel time was down to between eight and nine hours. Leaving Bandon at half past eight in the morning, he would reach Strasbourg at about half past three that afternoon.

For MEPs, flying is commuting, a wearing necessity which absorbs large chunks of valuable time. But no job is without its compensations. Being an MEP is lucrative. This is not principally for the salary, but for the expenses and allowances which go with the job. Irish MEPs receive a Dáil salary of almost £33,000, but a general expenditure allowance of about £2,264 a month is paid for office management costs, telephone, postage and travel. Each MEP must produce a contract of employment for their assistant or assistants, who are then paid a salary directly. The maximum amount which can be claimed for one or more assistants is just over £6,000 a month. MEPs are also paid a travel allowance and they receive a subsistence allowance of about £160 a night to cover the cost of accommodation and meals at their place of work in Brussels or Strasbourg. Brian responds to suggestions that he and other MEPs are riding a European 'gravy train' with some exasperation. 'On a purely financial level, if I was working and putting the amount of hours into a private business myself, I would be ten times wealthier than I am. I'd have ten times more money and far less hassle. I honestly believe that politicians are underpaid. I've seen it with my own family – the financial difficulty that we had as a family growing up because of the low level of pay.'

The plane dips over the flat Belgian countryside. In Brussels, traffic streams along the main arteries of the city. Rue Belliard, a steeply inclining street, is the location of the unremarkable, modern building in which Brian Crowley has his office. Any illusions of glamour evaporate in the functional, black-tiled entrance lobby, the decor reminiscent of an Irish regional technical college. Security staff – mostly women wearing black bomber jackets and grey trousers – check bags through a scanner. On one side of the lobby is a reception area where identification pictures can be produced in minutes by a camera stationed inside the counter.

Brussels' charm lies away from the functional architecture of the Rue Beillard, in the warren of narrow, cobbled streets and fine public buildings beyond the parliament blocks. Antique tiling, decorative plaster work and wrought-iron balustrades lend individuality to the three-storey houses in the side streets, where uniform rows are strikingly absent; instead there are cobbled squares and fountains. In the main tourist area, the Grand Place, restaurants mount elaborate displays of seafood, exotic fruit and vegetables on street tables; *choclatiers* emit the warm, sweet aroma of Belgium's famous chocolates. A chocolate lover, Brian purposely eats none of it when he is in Brussels; he's afraid he couldn't stop eating it if he started.

Brian Crowley has no great love for the city he lives in four days a week. 'The best buildings have been destroyed, except for the Grand Place area,' he says. 'There's no warmth about it at all.' When he goes out socially, he likes to go for a meal in an outlying town such as Bruges or meet up with some friends of his who play with bands in Antwerp.

There is an argument which says that people who are disabled are only disabled because society does not accommodate their needs. When Brian went looking for accommodation in Brussels, he found that only three hotels were accessible to him; all the others either had steps up to the entrance or doors that were too small. He found a place eventually in the Irish quarter, where many of the city's Irish pubs are located, most of them also inaccessible to the new arrival from Cork.

When he went to attend the parliament buildings in Brussels, Brian found the various sections interlinked on the upper levels by walkways similar to the airbridges at airports, but he encountered some difficulties in the buildings in Strasbourg. The month after he was elected, he went to Strasbourg to vote for a new president of the European parliament. Most votes in the parliament are taken by a show of hands or by electronic voting, but for positions such as president, the vote has to be by ballot. The ballot box was at the end of a flight of six steps. Brian managed to get down the steps but couldn't get back up again. He didn't get caught a second time. For the next ballot vote, he arranged for the ushers to bring the ballot box to where he was sitting. He did not think any major changes needed to be made to the building, though, because in the lifetime of the parliament, there may be only four ballot votes in five years.

His office in Belliard is an unprepossessing room, opening directly off a corridor. While he's going through the post, he dials RTE's phoneline news service and catches up with the latest developments at home. The office contains little furniture: two desks, two chairs and a filing cabinet. Among the post and files on his desk lie three books: the *Oxford Dictionary of Quotations*, *The Works of Oscar Wilde* and a selection Yeats' poems. A series of Martyn Turner cartoons hang on the wall behind his desk. One of them, dating from 1983, is called 'The Resumption of the Special Relationship After the Fianna Fáil Election'. It shows Charles Haughey sitting on a sofa while Margaret Thatcher, pouring tea from a pot with one hand, holds a hammer behind her back with the other. The caption reads: 'One lump or two?' Next to the cartoons is a postcard produced by Saoirse, the campaign for the release of Irish prisoners. Brian is wearing a green ribbon on the lapel of his jacket. He explains it stands for the release of all Irish political prisoners – loyalist and republican.

Brian works with three principal advisors; one of their main briefs is to alert him to any matters in the huge output of material emerging from the parliament which could have implications, positive or negative, for Ireland. Brian relies heavily on Denis Smyth, a quiet-mannered Dubliner with a moustache, who is advisor on social affairs and works principally with the

Social Affairs Committee. Frank Barrett from Clare is secretary general of the Fianna Fáil group, which is a member of the Union for Europe body in the parliament. Michael McGreil is advisor on regional affairs and fisheries.

Before 1979, the European parliament was a far less pressurised workplace for MEPs, who were appointed rather than elected and could afford to cruise in and out at will. They were also operating in a pre-Maastricht context where the powers of the parliament were very limited. However, the public perception of idle MEPs riding first class on the European gravy train is for the most part dated. The parliament has gained significant additional powers, and its member carry a heavy workload. They are answerable to their electorate and face pressure from their peers and from the media to perform well. Political opponents capitalise if they are not on top of their subject. There is pressure also from the many lobbyists who gather in Brussels to pursue their particular interests.

The parliament is a carousel of continuous meetings, voting and reports, but it is also difficult for an MEP to show results. To a large extent, it remains the 'poor relation' of the Commission or the Council of Ministers: MEPs cannot initiate legislation, though the parliament's increasing powers allow them much scope to amend new legislation. As a result, an MEP can spend almost eight hours in every week doing nothing but voting. There are thousands of votes to contend with: between 1990 and 1992, parliament proposed almost 2,500 amendments to introductory legislation, of which over 1,150 were accepted by the Council of Ministers. New powers also mean that the parliament plays a crucial role in the allocation of structural funds to EU member states and in determining European security and defence policy.

The most difficult aspect of the work Brian encountered at the start was the sheer range of material an MEP had to deal with. 'You had to learn very quickly to be discerning in what you had to know and what you didn't have to know. Besides that, the only other thing was trying to get a handle on people, to know the right people in the right places. That just comes with time more than anything else. I think I underestimated the amount of work that would be involved, and I would consider myself to be well-read, to have a fair degree of knowledge about it.'

His first task was to get to know the people within the Union for Europe group – the French, Portuguese, Greek and Italian members. He is not a fluent speaker of French but he 'gets by', and if anything urgent needs to be discussed, he uses an interpreter. Outside his own group, he put a lot of work into 'getting a handle on' members of the different committees on which he was serving.

'He's a good networker,' one parliament insider comments. 'He built up a good address and phone book. Someone must have advised him. Also, he's instantly recognisable which is helpful... He's friendly. People respond to that. If you are friendly, reserve breaks down quite easily. People are well-disposed towards Ireland here, and there are friendly faces in the Commission which can be helpful.'

Crowley had arrived in Brussels as a relatively inexperienced European politician. But while he faced new challenges to his ability, with different players and higher stakes than any he had previously experienced, the fundamentals of politics and of human nature were essentially the same, and he drew a great deal of confidence from that. 'In the Parliament,' he tells you, 'we're recognised as being the best dealers in the business.'

ON this September morning, the exam hall in UCC is charged with a tension particular to halls of its kind everywhere, the silence broken only by the clearing of a throat or the rustling of paper. Brian Crowley's summer has been split between Brussels and Strasbourg and the country roads of Munster, and for the first time since beginning his law course, he is not confident facing the papers. The election over, he started studying to do the exams in the autumn, but trying to squeeze in a few hours when he came home at night was difficult. Already, he had four or five functions to go to on any weekend.

The exam finished, Brian's attention turns to another set of papers – the newspapers carrying the story which has broken the evening before and which now dominated the media. On 31 August 1994 the IRA announced a cessation of its military campaign – to begin at midnight that night. As Brian read the news a wave of feeling washed over him. It seemed just then that the world *could* change for the better.

It was also the summit of his mentor Albert Reynolds' career as Taoiseach, but within months he was out of office, forced to resign in a controversy linked to the Attorney General's department. Later, when the ceasefire buckled and eventually collapsed, Brian Crowley felt cheated. He believed that the peace process lost its impetus when Albert Reynolds left government; that his successors failed to keep up the momentum towards peace, failed to hold the sides together.

Brian folded the newspaper and wheeled out of the university. It comes as no surprise to him to discover that he passed three exams, again with second-class honours, but failed the other papers. He realised that he had reached the end of the road in trying to reconcile studies with a political life and puts off completing his degree until a later stage. The energy he put into study and music would now be spent on the force that had driven him into Europe. Politics had finally gushed to the surface, sweeping all before it, and bobbing among the flotsam, fast-disappearing on the swell, was one battered leather jacket as Brian Crowley, MEP, faced into his new life.

Chapter Ten

WHEN DAWN GEARY began working for Brian, she found his manner brisk and businesslike. There was little casual conversation: he outlined what was needed and was off. Although she found his briskness disconcerting at first, she got used to it after a while, and in other ways he was easy to work for. He accepted the schedules she made out for him without demur and he did not get frayed with fatigue or snappy under pressure. His hectic days allowed little time for small-talk; he was always between meetings and running against time. His focus was simply on getting things done.

Brian Crowley fronts a tightly organised constituency operation. Dawn, his personal assistant, has responsibility for setting out his schedule, consulting sometimes with Niall Crowley, his programme manager, or Manus O'Callaghan, his special adviser. When Brian returns from Europe he faces a busy timetable. He may visit factories or meet with business people. He holds meetings with interest groups and constituents, alerting them to upcoming European programmes and sounding out their concerns about issues at local level. At the weekend, he would address a number of groups on Friday, keep appointments with constituents, community or interest groups on Saturday morning and open an exhibition or attend a function that evening. He tries to keep Sunday a free day, but often without success. Each Sunday night there is correspondance to deal with and letters to dictate. Dawn looks after the minutiae of the organisation, whether dealing with the volume of correspondance and communication that flows through Crowley's office or lining up a fork-lift to raise him on to a platform to open a festival. Working for an MEP has not made her a fan of his lifestyle. 'I wouldn't wish it on my worst enemy,' she says.

But Brian Crowley enjoys his life. He enjoys the power and recognition that comes with being an MEP, and likes the feeling of being able to make things happen. When he contacts an office or department, he can sense the change in attitude when the call is from an MEP. He gets the information he wants and he gets listened to. When he was a senator, he might hardly get acknowledged. 'It's an amazing thing for me to see,' he admits cheerfully. 'I suppose it's a human nature type of thing.'

There is a growing awareness of the influence European membership has on Irish life, particularly following the 1993 Maastricht Treaty, which committed the fifteen states to achieving a closer union and gave the commission and parliament greater authority to bring that about. But the scale of the European Union is so enormous that individuals can feel – and often are – lost in its vastness. Brian Crowley spends a lot of time talking about the relevance of what goes on in Europe. 'There is a lot of power emanating from Europe. In the last year or so, 40 per cent of the laws that have come into Ireland have come directly from Europe. They are laws that the Irish government did not change or could not change.' He hammers out this message in schools and 'information access meetings' with constituents and groups, aiming to bridge the gap in understanding between the European Union and its citizens.

Crowley has set up information offices throughout the constituency, but communicating with a broad electorate is difficult, both from a practical point of view and because the work of an MEP is often seen as being remote from people's daily interests. However, the impact of Europe continues to make itself felt, and people must and do respond to it. Young people are interested because they see job opportunities in Europe. The impact of structural funding is clearly visible and announced on billboards whenever road building projects or other urban or rural developments are aided by European funding. Community development groups who would previously have sought support nationally now look to programmes supported by European schemes and approach their MEP for advice. Social, cultural and community interest groups have begun to lobby Europe directly, as certain sectors, such as business and agriculture, have done for many years. Others have discovered the cost of not doing so. 'We have 16 per cent of EU water,' Foyle Fisherman's Co-op manager Dr Peter Tyndall points out, 'and we are entitled to under 5 per cent of the EU catch. Our politician don't even seem to realise we live on an island.'

In order to stay on top of his brief as an MEP, Brian Crowley has had to come to grips with a greater array of issues than he has ever previously dealt with. His friend Barry Slattery remarks that what Brian would have known about agriculture before becoming an MEP would have fitted on the back of a postage stamp, but now groups such as Teagasc acknowledge his expertise. He represents a constituency with some of the best farmland in Europe, a constituency with a vast and valuable coastline, a consituency with social and regional problems and potential. He has been learning as he goes along. A large part of his work is keeping up with the massive amount of information which crosses his desk, as many as thirty reports on different issues in any week, and keeping up communication with the people and bodies whose cases he represents. He looks up from a sheaf of papers on his desk. 'They never get information to MEPs quickly enough,' he says in annoyance. 'Even their lobby or representative groups who are supposed to be doing that don't get the information to us quick enough a lot of the time.'

His job is to stay tuned to the impact which European

legislation may have in his constituency. Though he is convinced of the benefits of EU membership, he is also very much
aware that it has its downside. He believes that the Common
Fisheries Policy has been disastrous and needs to be reformed,
'but no one seems to have the bottle to do it'. He has opposed
an EU directive which would 'liberalise' the postal services,
believing that if the proposal were implemented, it would result
in job losses and could mean the closure of rural post offices. He
points to the ridiculousness of 'these proposals coming forward
from the commission, when at the same time, another commissioner is giving money towards LEADER and towards rural
development, but yet you're taking away the very necessary basic
services that rural communities need to survive.'

Such contradictions are inevitable in the varied and complex
programmes which emanate from Brussels. As one member of
this enormous structure, Brian Crowley works the corridors of
Brussels and Strasbourg, joining the horse-trading and bargaining which takes place behind closed doors, in committee sessions and lobbies. One of his first moves was to seek a position
as co-ordinator of the Social Affairs and Employment
Committee. He won the support of his colleagues and found a
strong ally in Social Affairs Commissioner, Padraig Flynn. One
of the most important committees of the parliament, Social
Affairs is concerned with putting a social heart back into the
European Union, which has for so long focused on purely economic issues. It deals with policy areas of direct relevance to
Irish communities, whether establishing an action plan to deal
with drugs, creating a programme for the disabled, or promoting
small and medium sized enterprises. As co-ordinator, Brian's role
is to brief the fifty-seven other MEPs of his Group, to reconcile
their different views and prepare voting positions. A large
amount of the work is carried out not at official meetings but on
the fringes of the group, where deals are cut and differences
ironed out.

In common with all MEPs, he advances from committee to committee, keeping up with moving coalitions of interests. Inside parliament he is one MEP among 627 and to achieve anything he must network. As a member of the Legal Affairs Committee, Brian is well placed to brief himself on the issues before the parliament; almost every other committee seeks its opinion on forthcoming proposals. The Committee on Rules and Procedures has very little policy input of any kind, but as it oversees the inner working of the EU organisation, the advantage of membership is that you get to know how the place operates.

Crowley recalls a bid to introduce legislation on health and safety in the workplace, which would have required heavy works vehicles to be changed every five years. 'When I saw it, I thought: this is going to cost a fortune.' The proposal was voted down. Afterwards Brian discovered that the MEP sponsoring the measure represented a constituency with huge production plants for JCBs and tractors.

There is no publicity in overturning such a proposal because it comes from the commission into a committee of the parliament and never actually gets into the public domain. Other issues have brought with them the full glare of the media. Brian was one of a group of MEPs criticised for 'junketing' at a European conference in Guadalupe. His outburst in parliament, when he described a procedural decision as being as lacking in democracy as Hitler, earned angry rebukes from fellow MEPs. On the other hand, he was applauded in Strasbourg when he demanded that the president and the parliament express their outrage at the British authorities' handling of the stand-off between nationalists and loyalists in the north of Ireland in the summer of 1996.

He is noticeable in the European parliament as one of just two MEPs who use a wheelchair. In that respect he represents disabled people simply by being a disabled person himself, in spite of never campaigning as a 'disability candidate'.

'He doesn't want to be seen as somebody representing the

disabled,' Seamus Thompson, CEO of the Irish Wheelchair Association, says. 'I think he's right in that. There's no point in flying the disabled flag. He's doing it in a subtler way.' He thinks Brian's significance is to have gone ahead and achieved as much as any able-bodied person, to have shown that disabled people live a full, productive and satisfying life. 'He's a role model. The fellow has a lot of energy and anything he does, he does it well. He's not willing to be second best.'

'Disability is not really an issue with Brian. He's got a life and he's going to live it,' says Martin Naughton, one of the founder members of the Centre for Independent Living. 'While we admire Brian in that respect, we sometimes feel annoyed that he's not full-time committed to changing the world for people who are disabled, as we are.' Naughton feels that Brian should make the disability issue his priority, and thinks that he has a good deal to learn about how the rights and concerns of disabled people can be advanced.

Brian defends his record on disability issues in the European parliament: he is active in the Social Affairs committee's Helios programme for the disabled and the parliament's Disability Group, of which he is a member. Working through the Inter-Governmental Conference he has advocated a change to the Maastricht Treaty's anti-discrimination provisions so that discrimination would be assessed not alone in relation to race and sex, but also disability. Such a clause would mean that somebody could not be discriminated against by reason of their disability or their age under the different EU-funded programmes.

But not all aspects of this issue are covered by legislation; bringing disability to the public eye is important, especially when the disabled have been hidden from view for so long. Martin Naughton sees Brian as a catalyst in the changing perception of disabled people in Irish society. 'He bucked the system. He has not accepted any kind of passive dependency. He was Brian all the way through.'

Now that he is in the public eye, there are greater demands on him. As a young politician, topping the poll in Munster is both an achievement and a burden. There is pressure on him to sustain that vote. In politics, as Albert Reynolds might have told him, 'if you look after the voters, the voters will look after you'. Next time round, he will be judged by the electorate on his track record. There's a debt to be paid to the 84,463 people who ticked off his name on the ballot sheet.

Right now, he copes with the pressures of the job, enjoying the power and the prestige, the sense of being at the centre of what is happening. Europe is exciting, constantly growing and changing. The European parliament is attractive to him as a long term option because of its growing power. He has broad scope in dealing with issues he could never deal with at home. There is also the financial security of only having to seek re-election every five years. If he goes for a second term, he could climb the ladder of European office. 'I suppose it's a whole new world opened up for him,' his sister Fiona says. But these things change; politics, as Brian puts it, is 'very fluid'.

'You can only hold on to a seat as long as you work at it. It may be that when you do the very best you can and put your heart and soul into it that people will still reject you. But you know within yourself there was nothing more you could have done. That's the driving force.' That, and perhaps the memory of the hall in Clonakilty when his father was defeated.

Brian grew up with politics, was reared with it in the house. 'He is interested in politics,' Pat Fenton says of him, 'because politics is his life.' He has the kind of deep political shrewdness which comes from a background steeped in party affairs, yet at other times he can sound quite naive. 'I hear him say things on radio and television and I wince,' Dermot Clancy says, though he adds: 'He is a sincere politician in that he views politics not only as a means of providing him with a career but as a means of doing some good.' Brian does genuinely feel for people. He loves talking to people and working with people. But whether his compulsion is to try to improve the lot of others or an addiction to the party rooms, politics is in his blood. 'The first beat of the drum, like a native out in the jungle, you're away,' Dan Joe O'Mahony says of it. 'You might have made all the promises – never again! – but the first beat of the drum, you're off. Politics to us was a religion; it was very sacred and still is. You can't resist it.'

When Brian comes back to Bandon, he might sometimes go over to Shanley's, but usually there are functions or meetings to attend. 'It's all politics, politics,' Una O'Sullivan says. He has less space to live his own life, less time to spend with friends. Like friends everywhere, they've all drifted a little. Though Brian can often be the one to send a card or ring an old friend out of the blue, when Una O'Sullivan meets the guy she knew as the laid back singer with Galaxy, she finds it hard to talk to him. He's more serious, busy, directed; 'It's like he's totally, totally obsessed with the whole thing.' She recalls the days when she would ring him from work sometimes at two o'clock in the afternoon and he would still be in bed. 'He was so lazy, it's unbelievable.' Now he allows himself four days off at Christmas. His ambition for a summer holiday was to map out two weeks to have 'totally for doing nothing'. As it turned out, he took about five days. 'He's lost for time really, and ultimately it probably will take its toll,' Dermot Clancy says. 'I have suggested several times to him that it was time he developed some type of romance in his life. That is always greeted with a totally non-responsive look.'

Sometimes he goes over to babysit for Niall and his wife Adrienne. His nephew, young Brian, sits up on his lap and they wheel around in the wheelchair. Lately, young Brian has taken to asking his uncle to get out of the chair and allow him take a spin in it himself.

If any of his friends are around, Adrienne will ask Brian, 'How's Monique?' And Brian replies, 'Ah, she's fine.' The lads never know whether they're joking or not. Adrienne would love to see him with somebody, but she'd really have to be somebody special. 'Very understanding, for a start. She would very much have to be like him, very outgoing. But he just honestly doesn't have the time. He has so much going on.'

Brian enjoys being single. He is free to go places and to do things at will, free to take on a heavy workload. About half of his friends are married. He has been best man to Jim O'Driscoll and to his brothers Niall and Flor, and he is godfather to four children.

'I'd like to get married,' he says. 'I probably will when I meet the right person.' He would like the companionship of a partner, sharing a life with somebody; he would like to have a family as well. But he wouldn't be overly worried if he never got married, 'as long as I was happy with my life. I would hate to think that I would allow myself to get married just because I thought I should really get married at this stage and settle down.'

His schedule has not allowed anything deeper than a few casual dates since he became an MEP. He was involved with someone off and on for a few months and he occasionally goes out with women friends to the theatre or for a meal, but to have a steady relationship he would have to alter his lifestyle, and he's not prepared to do that at the moment. He wouldn't ask it of a partner, either. If or when Brian Crowley marries, his wife may have to accept a ready-made role as a political spouse. 'I think they would see that with their own eyes without having to explain it in explicit terms,' he says. At the same time, he expects that any woman would have her own career and her own rights. 'I would have to adjust my lifestyle to that. It's about compromise, about working things out.'

The loss of full physical sexuality is one of the biggest deprivations he has had to live with. 'As frustrating as it can be at times, it's not the end of the world either,' he says. 'There are more ways of sexually gratifying someone than through sexual intercourse alone – how many videos and books are there at the moment about massage and the art of erotic massage, therapeutic massage and everything like that? You enjoy the learning experience as well, finding what makes someone tick.' He does not know if his physical injuries have rendered it impossible for him to father children; he feels that, if he wants to have children, he will more than likely have to use an artificial method such as in vitro fertilisation. He looks on these as very relative difficulties. 'It's not something I think about a lot or dwell on. If I saw someone who was attractive, I would go for it and it wouldn't hold me back in that sense.'

He finds it difficult to talk about himself personally. It's easier to look at things in general terms, to talk politics. 'If a topic comes up for conversation, I can talk on it,' he says, 'but I'm not a great conversationalist.' More often, he is happy to sit on his own, reading a book or watching television, listening to music. The communicator with enough charisma to win the hearts and votes of virtual strangers, he can withdraw into himself to the point of seeming aloof. He likes his own company.

An amalgam of different and sometimes opposing personality traits, he is the private person who has surrendered his life to the public. With his long hair, he looks like a drummer from Def Leppard, yet he is opposed to divorce. A fast driver in a powerful car, he uses the silences of the journeys to pray occasionally. He has no reservations about expressing his devotion to Our Lady. Money is not a priority, but he can be flamboyant in spending it. He wants to buy a house near the sea, possibly in West Kerry. He has a share in a racehorse syndicate and has played blackjack in casinos in Guadaloupe, Paris, Portugal and London. 'The odds are more in your favour playing poker than they are in politics'.

He is not the best of timekeepers. He doesn't vent his anger in bursts of temper; rather, he goes quiet. Brian Crowley likes to be right. He likes to win, to succeed. Beneath the surface, there is a steely determination. He has a tremendous streak of stubbornness. He is sensitive, yet he can shut people out. Non-confrontational, he doesn't return fire with fire. Terminally addicted to politics and to music, he becomes most animated when talking about either.

Still a night owl, Brian sleeps into the day when his schedule allows. When he gets up to a new day, he spends ten to fifteen minutes rotating his ankles, knees and hips to encourage circulation and to keep his joints from locking. He has to watch his weight, mainly because it is harder to lift himself in and out of the chair or in and out of bed if he is heavy. The palms of his hands are calloused from pushing the chair.

The chair takes its toll on his suits as well, fraying the cuffs or catching the sleeves in the wheels. Obviously, shoes don't wear: the laces are the first things to go. He sometimes thinks of how he would look standing up – imagining the cut of a suit or the fall of a jacket when he buys something new. When he sees a bunch of kids playing football, he thinks it would be great to go over and kick a ball around with them. But he doesn't dwell on things that cannot be.

When he goes places, Brian talks about walking, not wheeling or pushing. He drives on his own. Hand controls attached to the steering column in his car are linked to the brake and the accelator by a cable. Once, when the connections snapped, he operated the controls with a baseball bat. Brian Crowley is used to improvising when it comes to getting where he wants to go.

'I don't agree that disabled people are different,' he says. 'I think we're equal and sometimes maybe even better. When I dream, I am often walking again, with absolutely no obstacles; and when I wake up to my reality, I still have no obstacles. That reality is my gift from God, and I thank him every day of my life.'